A NEW GUIDE TO SEX IN THE 21ST CENTURY

For the women who learned it the hard way

Louise Perry

A New Guide to Sex in the 21st Century

The Young Adult adaptation of
The Case Against the Sexual Revolution

polity

Copyright © Louise Perry 2025

The right of Louise Perry to be identified as Author of this Work has been asserted in accordance with the UK Copyright, Designs and Patents Act 1988.

The Case Against the Sexual Revolution first published in 2022 by Polity Press. This edition first published in 2025 by Polity Press.

Polity Press
65 Bridge Street
Cambridge CB2 1UR, UK

Polity Press
111 River Street
Hoboken, NJ 07030, USA

All rights reserved. Except for the quotation of short passages for the purpose of criticism and review, no part of this publication may be reproduced, stored in a retrieval system or transmitted, in any form or by any means, electronic, mechanical, photocopying, recording or otherwise, without the prior permission of the publisher.

ISBN-13: 978-1-5095-6280-0 (hardback)
ISBN-13: 978-1-5095-6281-7 (paperback)

A catalogue record for this book is available from the British Library.

Library of Congress Control Number: 2024933637

Typeset in 12 on 16pt Dante MT
by Cheshire Typesetting Ltd, Cuddington, Cheshire
Printed and bound in Great Britain by CPI Group (UK) Ltd, Croydon

The publisher has used its best endeavours to ensure that the URLs for external websites referred to in this book are correct and active at the time of going to press. However, the publisher has no responsibility for the websites and can make no guarantee that a site will remain live or that the content is or will remain appropriate.

Every effort has been made to trace all copyright holders, but if any have been overlooked the publisher will be pleased to include any necessary credits in any subsequent reprint or edition.

For further information on Polity, visit our website:
politybooks.com

CONTENTS

1 Sex must be taken seriously   1

2 Men and women are different   17

3 Not all desires are good   36

4 Loveless sex is not empowering   54

5 Consent is not enough   74

6 Violence is not love   87

7 People are not products   100

8 Marriage is good   119

Contents

Conclusion: Listen to Your Mother   140

Notes   145
Acknowledgements   164

SEX MUST BE TAKEN SERIOUSLY

Hugh Hefner found fame and success through founding porn magazine *Playboy*. Marilyn Monroe was a film star and model who became an icon of glamour and celebrity in the 1950s. They are both often seen as symbols of the sexual revolution.

What was the sexual revolution? It was a period that began in the 1960s when previous restrictive ideas around sex were relaxed or abandoned. These ideas included sex before and outside marriage being frowned upon, pornography being illegal or at least very hard to access, and so on. People became freer to do what they wanted when it came to sex. This process is often referred to as 'sexual liberation'.

Hefner and Monroe never met. They were, however, born in the same year and buried in the same place, side-by-side.[1] In 1992, Hefner bought the crypt next-door to Monroe's in the Westwood Memorial Park Cemetery in

Sex must be taken seriously

Los Angeles for $75,000.[2] He told the *Los Angeles Times* 'I'm a believer in things symbolic . . . [so] spending eternity next to Marilyn is too sweet to pass up.'[3]

At the age of ninety-one, Hefner got his wish. The long-dead Monroe had no say in the matter. But then, she had never been given much say in what men did to her over the course of her short life.

Marilyn Monroe was both the first-ever cover star and the first-ever naked centrefold in the first-ever edition of Hefner's *Playboy* magazine, published in December 1953. 'Entertainment for MEN' was the promise offered on the front cover, and the magazine evidently kept that promise, since it sold a *lot* of copies.

The magazine cover beckoned readers with the promise of a 'FULL COLOR' nude photo of the actress for the 'first time in any magazine'. Hefner later said that this centrefold was the key reason for the publication's initial success. Monroe herself was humiliated by the photoshoot. The photos had been taken four years earlier. She had them taken only because she was desperate for money at the time. She signed the release documents with a fake name.[4]

Hefner didn't pay her to use her images and didn't seek her consent before publishing them.[5] Monroe reportedly told a friend that she had 'never even received a thank-you from all those who made millions off a nude Marilyn photograph. I even had to buy a copy of the magazine to see myself in it.'[6]

The very different lives of Monroe and Hefner perfectly illustrate the nature of the sexual revolution's impact on

Sex must be taken seriously

men and women. Monroe and Hefner both began in obscurity and ended their lives rich and famous. They found success in the same city and at the very time in history. But while Hefner lived a long, grubby life in his mansion with his many girlfriends (or 'playmates'), Monroe died, miserable and alone, from a drug overdose, aged just thirty-six. Exploited by a series of seedy men like Hefner, her life was plagued by unhappy relationships and poor mental health.

Monroe's life followed a similar path to that of the pop star Britney Spears. In 1999, at the age of sixteen, she gyrated in a school uniform and begged viewers to 'hit me baby, one more time'. Spears has since suffered a very public nervous breakdown. She is like many others who have been destroyed in much the same way as the original icon of sexual freedom, Marilyn Monroe.

The public asks a lot of the women it desires; women like Marilyn Monroe and Britney Spears. And, when it all goes horribly wrong, as it usually does, this public labels these once-desired women 'crazy' and moves on. Difficult questions about whether 'sexual liberation' is to blame for destroying women like this are never asked.

Hugh Hefner experienced sexual liberation very differently from Monroe. As a younger man, he was the true playboy – handsome, charming, and envied by other men. He lived the fantasy of a particularly immature teenage boy. He hosted parties for his celebrity friends in a garish 'grotto' and then retired upstairs with his gang of identical twenty-something blondes. He supposedly once said that his best

Sex must be taken seriously

pick-up line was simply the sentence 'Hi, my name is Hugh Hefner.'[7] He lived to a ripe old age.

Hefner certainly never experienced any guilt for the harm he perpetrated. Asked at the age of eighty-three if he regretted any of the 'dark consequences' of the *Playboy* revolution he set in motion, Hefner was confident in his innocence: 'it's a small price to pay for personal freedom'.[8] By which he meant, of course, personal freedom for men like him.

After his death in 2017, many newspapers and websites argued that he had helped feminism because he supported things like legalising abortion and making the contraceptive pill widely available. These developments were crucial in ensuring that women could have sex without risking pregnancy. Without them, the sexual revolution could not have happened.

But Hefner did not support these things because he wanted to help women. Hefner never once campaigned for anything that didn't bring him direct benefit. Getting rid of the risk of pregnancy merely took away one of the reasons why women might refuse to have sex with him.

Before the sexual revolution, women had limited options when it came to sex. One option was to not have sex. Another was to get married and have children. The final one was to have sex without being married, but risk terrible consequences: getting pregnant and becoming a social outcast. It is true that the sexual revolution means that women have more choices now.

But there was a lot more to it than that. The invention of the Pill did free many women from unwanted

Sex must be taken seriously

childbearing. But the likes of Hefner also wanted this technology, and needed it, so they could indulge their own sexual desires. They still do so, often in ways that harm women, while pretending that they are liberating them.

The Pill

The impact of the contraceptive pill [the Pill] was vast. There have been plenty of periods in human history in which the norms around sex have been loosened, but their impact was limited because reliable contraception did not exist. Sex outside marriage risked pregnancy. So, straight men in pursuit of extramarital sex mostly had to seek out sex either with prostitutes, or with the small number of eccentric women who were willing to risk being cast out permanently from respectable society.

But the sexual revolution of the 1960s was a much bigger deal. It permanently changed things, and now we're so used to it that we barely notice. It was able to happen because of the arrival, for the first time in the history of the world, of reliable contraception and, in particular, forms of contraception that women could take charge of themselves. These included the Pill, the diaphragm, and subsequent improvements on those technologies.

They meant that, at the end of the 1960s, an entirely new creature arrived in the world: the apparently fertile young woman, whose fertility had in fact been put on hold. She changed everything.

Sex must be taken seriously

This process clearly had its benefits, but should we see it purely as a good thing? I don't think so. This is because the sexual revolution has not, in fact, freed *all* of us. It has freed *some* of us, and at a price. Which is exactly what we should expect from such a massive change. However, the most popular story told about this revolution – the one told by political liberals and progressives – does not recognise this complexity. It sees the sexual revolution as a story only of progress.

I know this because I used to believe it. As a younger woman, I held the same political opinions as most other educated urban millennials in the West. I was a liberal feminist who believed that sexual freedom was a straightforwardly good thing with no downsides. I eventually changed my mind, in part because of my own life experiences, including a period immediately after university spent working at a rape crisis centre (more on this in the next chapter).

When I say 'liberal feminist', I mean a particular kind of feminism that has become dominant in the last generation or so. This kind of feminism prioritises freedom above everything else. For instance, when the actress and prominent liberal feminist Emma Watson was criticised in 2017 for showing her breasts on the cover of *Vanity Fair,* she hit back with a well-worn liberal feminist phrase: 'feminism is about giving women choice . . . It's about freedom.'[9]

For Watson and her allies, that might mean the freedom to wear revealing clothes (and sell lots of magazines in the process), or the freedom to sell sex, or make or consume porn, or pursue whatever career you like, just like the boys.

Sex must be taken seriously

Liberal feminism promises women freedom. But female biology imposes, in reality, limits on that freedom. Women get pregnant, and being pregnant and having children is not compatible with complete freedom. When this becomes clear, liberal feminism supports trying to break those limits by using money, technology, and the bodies of poorer people. For example, it says that women should employ a full-time nanny so that they can work very long hours rather than look after their child.

I don't reject the desire for freedom. I'm not an anti-liberal. Goodness knows that women have every reason to be unhappy about many of the limits placed on them, both now and in the past. However, I am critical of any political worldview that fails to balance freedom against other good things. Women don't only seek freedom. They want other things, and we need to bear this in mind and ask whether sexual freedom might stop them from getting some of these other things.

In this book I'm going to ask – and seek to answer – some questions about freedom that liberal feminism can't or won't answer. Why do so many women desire a kind of sexual freedom that so obviously benefits men more than women? What do we lose when we prioritise freedom above all else? And, above all, *how should we act*, given all this?

I start from a position that historically many feminists have disliked. I accept the fact that men and women are different. They have different goals and interests. Those differences aren't going away. When we recognise these

Sex must be taken seriously

differences, then sexual politics takes on a different character. Instead of asking 'how can we all be free?', we must ask instead 'how can we best promote the wellbeing of both men and women, given that these two groups have different sets of interests, which are sometimes in tension?'

Sexual disenchantment

In this book, I'm going to argue that, in the modern West, our sexual attitudes and behaviour – our sexual 'culture' – doesn't properly balance these interests. It promotes the interests of creepy or predatory men like Hugh Hefner at the expense of women. And the influence of liberal feminism means that too many women don't recognise this. This suits men like Hugh Hefner very nicely, since playboys like him have a lot to gain from the new sexual culture. It is in their interests to support a very radical idea about sex that came out of the sexual revolution.

This is the idea that sex is nothing more than a leisure activity, only invested with meaning if the participants choose to give it meaning. Proponents of this idea argue that sex has no intrinsic specialness. It is not essentially different from, say, getting a haircut or eating a meal at a restaurant. This implies that it can be treated as something to be bought and sold, like anything else. This process is called 'sexual disenchantment'. It is the stripping away of the idea that sex is 'special', that it means something important and unique.

Sexual disenchantment is a natural consequence of the liberal privileging of freedom over all other values. If you

Sex must be taken seriously

want to be utterly free, you have to try to get rid of any kind of social restrictions that limit you. The most important one is the belief that sex has some unique specialness that is difficult to rationalise. When we get rid of this idea, there may be some benefits, but there is a huge downside. That downside hurts women disproportionately, for biological reasons that I'll come back to in the next chapter. It also creates a lot of confusion.

This confusion is well illustrated by the #MeToo movement.

This was a campaign that started in 2017. Many women began to talk about the fact that they had been sexually mistreated by men. They had previously not talked about these things because they were ashamed. The idea of #MeToo was to speak out so that something could be done about these abuses.

The stories that came out of #MeToo included plenty of straightforwardly criminal behaviour. However, there were also a lot of women who described sexual encounters that were technically legal and consensual, but nevertheless left them feeling terrible because they were being asked to treat as meaningless something that they felt to be meaningful.

One student wrote for instance of hooking up with one of her peers:

He slid inside me and I didn't say a word. At the time, I didn't know why. Maybe I didn't want to feel like I'd led him on. Maybe I didn't want to disappoint him. Maybe I just didn't want to deal with the 'let's do it,

Sex must be taken seriously

but no, we shouldn't' verbal tug-of-war that so often happens before sleeping with someone. It was easier to just do it. Besides, we were already in bed, and this is what people in bed do. I felt an obligation, a duty to go through with it. I felt guilty for not wanting to. I wasn't a virgin. I'd done this before. It shouldn't have been a big deal – *it's just sex* – so I didn't want to make it one.[10]

'It's just sex' summarises the sexual disenchantment idea perfectly.

This young woman wasn't beaten and she didn't get pregnant. She actually quite liked the young man she had sex with, at least at first. So why did she experience this sexual encounter as such a big deal? Because sexual disenchantment isn't actually true, and we all know it, including the liberal feminists.

You can tell this because when it became clear, during the #MeToo campaign, that the Hollywood producer Harvey Weinstein had been offering women career opportunities in exchange for sexual favours, these same liberal feminists immediately condemned him. They condemned him not only for the violence and threats he had used in the course of committing his crimes, but also for requesting sexual favours from his subordinates in the first place.

They instinctively recognised that asking for sex from an employee is not at all the same as asking them to do overtime or make coffee. I've made plenty of coffees for various employers in the past, despite the fact that coffee-making

Sex must be taken seriously

wasn't included in my job description, and I'm sure many readers will have done the same. While that was sometimes annoying, no worker who makes coffee for their boss will expect to end up dependent on drugs or alcohol as a consequence. No one will expect to become pregnant or acquire a disease that causes infertility. No one will expect to suffer from Post Traumatic Stress Disorder or other mental illnesses. No one will expect to become incapable of having healthy intimate relationships for the rest of her life. All of these things might happen if you have unwanted sex.

Everyone knows that having sex is not the same as making coffee and, when the idea of sexual disenchantment demands that we pretend otherwise, the result is a lot of muddle. Although at one level they sort of know that sex *is* special, liberal feminists are so committed to the idea of sexual freedom they have to find ways of trying to resolve this contradiction.

Perhaps, they ask, the problem is that we're not free enough? That the sexual revolution has had downsides only because it hasn't gone far enough? Maybe we still hold onto our shame too much? If we truly embraced total sexual hedonism, maybe it would all be ok? Liberal feminists therefore argue for more and more freedom and are continually surprised when the cure they support doesn't cure the disease.

This fact becomes clear when we look at modern universities, where the gospel of sexual liberation is preached loudest. At the beginning of term, freshers are typically given a lecture on the importance of consent and sent on

Sex must be taken seriously

their way with 'I heart consent' badges and tote bags. The rule they're taught is simple enough: with consent, anything goes. And yet, this simple rule is broken again and again, both through rape and also through the more subtle ways that men force women to do things they don't really want to do. Few liberal feminists are willing to draw the link between the culture of sexual hedonism they promote and the anxieties over campus rape that have emerged at exactly the same time.

If they did, they might be forced to recognise that they have done a terrible thing in advising inexperienced young women to do dangerous things. Things like being alone and drunk with horny men who are not only bigger and stronger than they are, but who have probably watched a lot of porn: the sort of porn that normalises aggression, coercion, and pain.

But, in liberal feminist circles you're not supposed to talk about the influence of online porn, or hook-up culture, or any of the other negative elements of our new sexual culture. To do so would be to question the doctrine of sexual freedom, which they refuse to do. So, young women are forced to learn for themselves that freedom has costs, and they are forced to learn the hard way, every time.

Chronological snobbery

Once I started writing this book, I soon realised that it wasn't enough simply to point out what is wrong with our sexual attitudes and behaviour. I soon realised that I would

Sex must be taken seriously

also need to offer readers some real guidance on how to live – but not the sort of silly advice that you find at the back of a glossy magazine. *Having* sex should be taken seriously, and so should *talking* about it. It's a serious matter.

The advice I'm offering applies almost exclusively to heterosexuals, particularly heterosexual women, because the effect of the sexual revolution on relations between the sexes is the subject of this book. Most of the advice I offer would have seemed like common sense until very recently. It's the sort of advice that your grandmother would think was very obvious. It is, however, advice that I know I often ignored.

Why did I ignore it? Because I was raised in an era when a simplistic story of history as always being 'progressive' was taken for granted. The problem with this story is that it encourages us to ignore both the ways in which things may have become worse over time, and also the advice offered by older generations. In 1955, the writer C. S. Lewis coined the phrase 'chronological snobbery' to describe:

> [T]he uncritical acceptance of the intellectual climate of our own age and the assumption that whatever has gone out of date is on that count discredited.[11]

Older people are dismissed by snobbish twenty-first century liberals as not only foolish and uninteresting, but also (far worse) as 'problematic'. While in most cultures the elderly are regarded as sources of wisdom and thus granted particular respect, in the modern West they are more likely

Sex must be taken seriously

to be ignored and assumed to be of no use to anyone. But maybe they are more worth listening to than we assume.

The fact is that in recent decades we have broken very dramatically with the past. The necessity of this break is constantly justified in the progressive media through reference to the bad-old-days. We tend to caricature the past to justify where we are now. But the reality is that things aren't that simple. There are downsides both to how things were in the past and how things are now. Highlighting the evils of the past also serves to distract from the evils of the present. Today, the way progressives represent life in the 1950s serves this purpose.

In 2016, an extract from a 1950s home economics book offering 'tips to look after your husband' went viral on social media. The housewife was advised that when her husband got home from work she should have dinner on the table, her apron off, a ribbon in her hair, and that she should always make sure to let her husband 'talk first'.[12] This advice was not unusual for housewife manuals of the time, or indeed those of earlier eras.

How 'problematic', we think now, how stupid and backwards! But, then, take a look at a small sample of *Cosmopolitan* magazine guides published within the last decade: '30 Ways to Please a Man',[13] '20 Ways to Turn On Your Man',[14] or 'How to Turn Him On – 42 Things to Do With a Naked Man'.[15] In what sense are these guides not encouraging precisely the same degree of prioritising male desires? The difference is that the focus is now on sexual desires rather than domestic comfort.

Sex must be taken seriously

Women are still expected to please men and to make it look effortless. But, while the 1950s 'angel of the house' hid her apron, the modern 'angel of the bedroom' hides her pubic hair. She pretends to orgasm, pretends to like anal sex, and pretends not to mind when the 'friends with benefits' arrangement causes her pain.

I've spoken to women who suffered from vaginismus for years without telling their partners that being penetrated was excruciating. I've also spoken to women who have had abortions after hook-ups and never told the men who impregnated them. While sharing the inside of their bodies was expected, revealing the inconvenient fact of their fertility felt too intimate. We have smoothly gone from one form of feminine subservience to another, but we pretend that we are now free. We're not.

Pretending that this is the case hurts the women like Marilyn Monroe, particularly when they are poor and friendless. I want above all in this book to speak to the young women who have been lied to by liberal feminism and so risk following a very, very dangerous example.

But the would-be Hugh Hefners are also hurt by the pretence, albeit in a less obvious way. Unlike Monroe, Hefner lived to grow old and, as he did so, he lost much of his glitter. By the end of his life, he was more often publicly portrayed as a pathetic figure. Various former playmates provided the press with unflattering accounts of life in the Playboy Mansion. The women spoke of soiled mattresses, and carpets covered with dog faeces.[16] It was also revealed that Hefner took an obsessive and bullying attitude towards

Sex must be taken seriously

his many girlfriends.[17] He became little more than a dirty old man.

Mouldering away in the Playboy Mansion doesn't kill a person, but it does corrode their soul. True happiness is not to be found on a soiled mattress, having sex with a woman who doesn't even like you. Liberalism flatters us by telling us that our desires are good, and that we can find meaning in satisfying them, whatever the cost. But the lie of this flattery should be obvious. Most of us have surely realised, once it's too late, that we were wrong to desire something. We realise that we hurt ourselves, or hurt other people, in pursuing it.

So I am going to propose an alternative form of sexual culture, one that recognises something more than our own desires. One that sees other human beings as real people, invested with real value and dignity.

It's time for a sexual counter-revolution.

MEN AND WOMEN ARE DIFFERENT

A Natural History of Rape by Randy Thornhill and Craig T. Palmer is not a book that feminists are supposed to like.[1] It isn't even a book that feminists are supposed to read. Followings its publication in 2000, the authors of the book were not only loudly criticised, but received so many death threats that they were advised by the police to regularly check their cars for bombs.[2]

But, when I first came across the book, I read it compulsively, all in one sitting, and was left by the end feeling both gloomy and oddly satisfied. I was working at the time at a rape crisis centre. My job was to help women and girls who had been raped, but I also trained volunteers for our helpline and went into schools to teach consent workshops. Consent workshops are lessons where young people are taught about what it means to properly agree to have sex with someone else. I was expected to base these lessons on

Men and women are different

a particular set of ideas about what rape is and why it happens.

These ideas were outlined most famously in a classic feminist book published in 1975 called *Against Our Will*, written by Susan Brownmiller. It was written during what is called the 'second wave' of feminism. This was a period after the most basic rights – such as the right to vote or to own property – had been won for women, but many injustices continued to exist, particularly in relation to things like sex, the family and work. The book had many positive effects; for example, it helped to convince many people that rape between a husband and wife should be illegal (which it hadn't been in many countries before). It had important flaws, however.

The general argument of the book was that rape happens because of something called 'the patriarchy'. This is the idea that our society is organised to give greater priority to men and their wishes than to women. In such a society, men have almost all the power and money, and view women as beings that exist purely to serve them, including sexually. Brownmiller argued that men become rapists because of the patriarchal society they live in and their upbringing – what is called their 'socialisation'. Rape in turn helps to ensure that women fear male power and violence, and so ensures that the patriarchy continues: it is an expression of political dominance. This is why the vast majority of rapes are committed by men against women. And so – goes this argument – to end rape, we must first end patriarchy.

Men and women are different

This idea of rape has become very popular among feminists of all different kinds. It implies that rape is not really about biology. Men do not rape because they are sexually attracted to a woman or have strong sexual urges. They rape because of – and as a way of upholding – their political dominance. This is often summarised in a popular phrase: 'rape is about power, not sex'.

I often repeated this view as a rape crisis worker – in fact, I probably used the exact phrase. I felt that to say otherwise – to suggest that rapists are motivated by sexual desire, not just a desire for control – would be to excuse them. Given that I was daily witnessing the terrible and lasting harm done by rape, of course I didn't want to do that. Plus, there really is some truth to the claim. For example, sexual harassment in the workplace is almost never perpetrated by junior men against more senior women. In the vast majority of cases, it is committed by those with more power against those with less.

But I realise now that I wanted to believe in the 'rape is about power' argument largely because I found the alternative theory about why men rape too depressing for words. What is this alternative theory, the one outlined by the dangerous book that we mentioned at the beginning of this chapter, *A Natural History of Rape*?

In short, it is the idea that men rape women because, on average, there are differences between men and women that are the result of evolution. Men have evolved to be generally more aggressive, and more prone to try to have as much sex with as many people as possible. The reason that rape is

Men and women are different

almost always committed by men against women – rather than the other way round – is because men evolved to be more violent and more horny. A minority of men will have these qualities to such a significant extent that they will rape.

Many feminists – including Susan Brownmiller – do not like this theory, for two reasons. They argue that if a tendency to rape women is a result of biology, then it could be seen to be permissible. They also argue that it implies that rape is inevitable: it will always happen.

This first reason is a textbook example of what philosophers call 'the naturalistic fallacy': the false belief that because something is natural it must necessarily be good. The belief that because it is 'natural' for men to rape, it must be justified is simply not true. It is 'natural' to die of smallpox: that doesn't mean that it is a good thing, and that we shouldn't vaccinate ourselves against it.

But the second claim is more difficult. If rape is indeed a product of evolution, does that make it inevitable? Well, not necessarily, but it certainly does make it more difficult to eradicate, which is, I think, a key reason for the historical reluctance of feminists to accept the 'biological' view of rape. Instead, most feminists continue to favour socialisation theory as the preferred way of explaining male and female behaviour, both good and bad. 'Socialisation theory' insists that there are no 'natural' differences between men and women, and that any differences we observe must be the product not of the fact that we are biologically different, but of the fact that we are treated differently from childhood (we are 'socialised' differently).

Men and women are different

It's true that adults treat little boys and little girls differently from the moment a child is born and we don't know exactly how much of an effect that different treatment has in the long term. However, it seems highly likely that it does have *some* effect and that differences between the sexes are therefore at least partially the result of socialisation. This is why feminists in recent decades have often paid close attention to how babies and small children are bought up by their parents. They often object to toys or advertising that promote gender stereotypes (giving girls toy ovens and hoovers and boys toy cars and chemistry sets, for example).

Many feminists have, however, taken this idea further. They insist that *all* the differences we see between men and women are the product of socialisation. Therefore, we could eliminate all such differences if we changed how we treated children. If we raised children differently, then within one generation we could completely remake the world. It's a nice idea, and I used to sincerely believe in it. But the evidence put forward by the authors of a *A Natural History of Rape*, as well as many other scientists, forces us to reckon with a possibility that is a lot less appealing: what if it's not that easy?

Human animals

Brownmiller writes in *Against Our Will* that 'no zoologist, as far as I know, has ever observed that animals rape in their natural habitat, the wild'.[3] But this statement is simply wrong. Plenty of other animals commit rape, and also

Men and women are different

behave in all of the other horrible ways in which human beings sometimes behave. The truth is that human beings are animals, and our minds and bodies have both been subject to the process of evolution by natural selection. This is the almost universally accepted theory of how animal species have come to be the way they are, proposed in the nineteenth century by Charles Darwin.

Like other animals, we sometimes demonstrate kindness, gentleness and friendliness. At other times we kill, torture and rape. And, just like other members of the Great Ape family, male and female members of our species are different in certain important ways – both in terms of our physical make-up and our behaviour.

Let's start with the physical side. Adult women are approximately half as strong as adult men in the upper body, and two-thirds as strong in the lower body.[4] On average, men can punch two-and-a-half times harder than women.[5] In hand grip strength, 90 per cent of females produce less force than 95 per cent of males.[6] In other words, almost all women are weaker than almost all men. Any feminist theory about the relationship between men and women has to recognise this fact. And men can out-run women, as well as out-punch them. Sex differences are less marked in sports that favour endurance, rather than strength alone, but are nevertheless large.

In Olympic swimming and track events, women's performances hover at around 90 per cent of men's, a figure sometimes referred to as the 'golden ratio' of athletics.[7] This may sound minor, but it translates into huge differences

Men and women are different

among the best athletes. At the 2016 Summer Olympics, for instance, Elaine Thompson of Jamaica won gold with a winning time of 10.71 seconds. In the same games, Usain Bolt, also of Jamaica, won with a time of 9.81 seconds. Although there was less than a second's difference between these two athletes, if men and women had been running in the same event, then Thompson wouldn't even have made it into the final race. In fact, she would have been easily out-run by Jamaican boys competing in the under-seventeen category.[8] The women's category has traditionally been protected in elite sports because if it were not protected, there would be no women in elite sports – men would defeat them every time.

But, recognising these kinds of physical limitations does not sit well with most modern feminism, which tends to oppose all restrictions on human freedom. If we acknowledge that there are unchangeable differences between the sexes in terms of strength and speed, then we are also forced to acknowledge that women experience a permanent physical disadvantage (and not just in sport). Freedom is not much good to you if you are always at a natural disadvantage. And, in the modern West, it has become increasingly possible to deny the existence of these physical differences: many people nowadays neither perform hard physical work nor bear children. But the unwelcome truth will always remain, whether or not we want to face it: almost all men can kill almost all women with their bare hands, but not vice versa. And that matters.

Men and women are different

Differences above the neck

Recognising these evolved bodily differences tends to be less controversial than also recognising that there are evolved psychological differences too. This may be because it's very easy to hear 'men and women are *on average* a certain way' and understand this to mean 'men and women are *always like this*', which anyone with any experience of the world will know is not true.

There are lots of men and women who are physically dissimilar from other members of their sex, and very many more who don't fit masculine or feminine stereotypes in terms of their interests and behaviour. In fact, I'd go further, and suggest that almost no one is a walking gender stereotype – I have some stereotypically feminine traits, and some stereotypically masculine ones, and I'm sure you do too.

But this kind of anecdotal evidence does not disprove the claim that there are some important average differences between the sexes, and that at the level of the entire population these differences have an effect. We can insist simultaneously that there are plenty of exceptions to the rule, and moreover that there is *nothing wrong* with being an exception to the rule, while also acknowledging the existence of the rule. The complication is that we are in one particular way different from all other species: we are uniquely intelligent. This means that, unlike other animals, we can choose to go against our instincts, at least to some extent. Also, unlike other animals, we have been able to spread ourselves

Men and women are different

across the planet and adjust to all kinds of different environments and places.

This variation can sometimes cause human societies to develop in very different directions. For instance, in a few cultures, mating customs look strange to us. The Na in China are famous for having no institution of marriage and deliberately preventing couples being in long-term relationships, and a few Amazonian groups believe that a child can have two or more biological fathers. The unusual mating customs of the twenty-first West – the subject of this book – are the product, not of climate or terrain, but rather of new technologies not available to people in the past, as I argued in Chapter 1.

But all of this variation it built upon a biological basis. Only one half of the human race is capable of getting pregnant, and – failing the invention of artificial wombs – this will remain true indefinitely. What's more, even if we were somehow to remove the human body entirely from reproduction, we would still be left with our human brains, which are also products of our evolution. The effects of evolution on psychological differences between men and women are controversial for a very good reason. The existence of such differences *can* be misused to make anti-feminist arguments. Blatant sexists can use the naturalistic fallacy to argue that unfair gender stereotypes are 'natural' and therefore good.

For example, in 2020, Will Knowland, an English teacher at Eton College – the oldest and poshest school in the UK – attracted a great deal of media attention when he was

Men and women are different

dismissed for producing a video titled 'The Patriarchy Paradox' as part of a course on critical thinking intended for older students.[9] Knowland used evolutionary biology to argue that women are both inherently inferior to men (not only smaller and weaker, but also less creative and innovative), and also that men have been uniquely victimised throughout human history, while women have been coddled.

Indeed, the fear that evolutionary theory will be used to make such sexist arguments means that the *very idea* of there being evolved psychological differences between the sexes has become taboo among many feminists. Although this is understandable, we should not respond to the misuse of science by rejecting science altogether. The science of evolution does not have an in-built political bias. It can be used for all sorts of political reasons, including to advance the feminist cause. *A Natural History of Rape* hit me like a ton of bricks because it alerted me to the feminist potential of evolutionary psychology, an area I had previously rejected as inherently suspect.

Rape and evolution

I sought out *A Natural History of Rape* because I was bothered by certain questions that conventional feminism couldn't answer. Why, for instance, are such a high proportion of rape victims teenagers?

My own experience of working with victims, as well as academic research, confirms what I suspected to be the

Men and women are different

case: the risk of a woman being raped increases very rapidly after the age of about twelve and decreases again, almost as rapidly, after the age of about thirty. The very young and the very old are sometimes raped, but this is rare: the most common age at which girls are raped is fifteen,[10] and less than ten per cent of rape victims are older than thirty.[11]

Could it really be a coincidence, I wondered, that the age of peak rape victimisation is also the age at which I personally attracted the most sexual harassment on the street? It turns out this isn't a coincidence, as the sociologists Richard Felson and Richard Moran write:

> Social science has demonstrated a strong relationship between age and sexual attractiveness. Heterosexual men are sexually attracted to young women, while homosexual men are attracted to young men. The age preference explains why adult film stars, sex workers, exotic dancers as well as glamour models are often young, and why their earnings decline as they age.[12]

Female rape victimisation and female sexual attractiveness peak at exactly the same age – the two graphs map onto each other almost perfectly. Socialisation theory can't account for this because, if 'rape is about power, not sex', why would rapists just happen to target the age group that also just happens to be the most sexually desirable to men?

And then there's the age of the rapists themselves. Although this skew isn't quite as extreme as it is among female victims, it's still very clear that most rapists are

Men and women are different

young men. One typical study found 46 per cent of rapists to be under age twenty-five, 17 per cent under age eighteen, and 15 per cent under age fifteen.[13] This fits not only with the usual age range of violent offenders in general – who are overwhelmingly young men – but also with the peak of male sex drive.[14] Again, if 'rape is about power, not sex', why would this be the case?

There was another issue that I had been having doubts about when I first opened *A Natural History of Rape*. In victim surveys, the proportion of rape victims who are male is typically somewhere between two and five per cent, with almost all of these rapes committed by other men. It occurred to me that this is about the same proportion of the male population that identifies as gay or bisexual. Is this a coincidence? Perhaps, but it seems unlikely, given that gay and bisexual men commit rape about as often as straight men do, but the victims of these rapists, of course, include other men and boys. Given these facts, should we still understand rape to be an expression of male political dominance over women rooted in patriarchy, or should we instead consider a much more obvious possibility: that rape is an aggressive expression of sexual desire?

Resistance to this research evidence comes from two very different groups, both of whom tend to either ignore the data or quibble with it. They often end up – perversely – sounding very similar. The first is the anti-feminist men's rights activists. The second is those feminists who, in an effort to be as inclusive as possible, deliberately avoid making any generalisations about either rapists or their victims. A rape

Men and women are different

crisis colleague, for instance, used to use the phrase 'people of all genders sexually assault people of all genders' while teaching workshops. This statement is technically true, but is very misleading, given that the vast majority of rapes and sexual assaults are committed by men against women.

In every part of the world, around 98 to 99 per cent of convicted sex offenders are male, and the women who make up the remaining one to two per cent typically offend quite differently. For instance, women are much more likely to offend alongside another person (usually a husband or boyfriend), and women almost never assault strangers. This is not to say that there are zero examples of women committing stranger rape or other crimes more typical of men, but it is foolish to pretend that there is not a very obvious pattern here.

No, I'm afraid that rape is a male crime, and not only in our species, but also in many others. And it has evolved for a startlingly obvious reason: because, in some circumstances, it can increase a man's chance of reproducing and passing on his genes. This is, in the end, what natural selection is all about.

The authors of *A Natural History of Rape* decided to apply this insight to the task of understanding the causes of rape and the best methods of preventing it. They began by stating an obvious fact: reproduction places more physical demands on women than it does on men. Pregnancy lasts more than nine months, and is followed by a dangerous labour, which is followed by many more years of breast-feeding and infant care.

Men and women are different

Men, however, only really *need* to expend the amount of effort it takes to orgasm in order to reproduce. It may also be advantageous for fathers to hang around after conception and increase the mother and baby's chances of survival, but it isn't always necessary. A man who can game the system by abandoning a woman after impregnating her, and then riding off into the sunset to impregnate many more women, is also successfully spreading his genetic material. He carries the risk of retribution, including violence from the woman's male family members, but in some instances the benefits may outweigh the risks. Put differently, there are different ways that male sexuality can work: the way that encourages commitment, and the way that encourages promiscuity (much more on this in Chapter 6).

When it was first published, *A Natural History of Rape* attracted a great deal of criticism from feminists, some of whom misrepresented the contents of the book.[15] Many critics misunderstood the argument that was being made. Others refused to accept that the authors were sincere in their condemnation of rape, despite the fact that there were very good reasons to think that they were. Too few of these feminist critics recognised how useful the book could be in helping to prevent rape. I strongly believe that this hostility to evolutionary psychology is a mistake, which is why, in the rest of this book, I'm going to regularly use the work of evolutionary psychologists in the course of making feminist arguments – once we accept that men and women are different, many other things follow.

Men and women are different

How to bear it

What proportion of men have the desire to rape? Not all, I'm happy to report, although the proportion is still disturbingly high. When asked in surveys, a minority of men typically say that they might hypothetically force an unwilling person into sex in some circumstances. A smaller minority admit to having done so in the past. In other words, there is a core minority who will be sexually aggressive in most circumstances, and a larger minority who will be sexually aggressive in some circumstances. This still means, thankfully, that the majority of men are not potential rapists.

But, unfortunately, it's not easy for potential victims to identify them. It is sometimes possible to spot rapists, or at least to make generalisations about them. For instance, in terms of personality, rapists tend to be more impulsive, hostile, disagreeable, promiscuous, hyper-masculine, and low in empathy compared with other men.[16] But appearances can always be deceptive.

So, how to avoid them? Most feminists dislike this question, and I do understand why. Every now and again, a police force will release some kind of campaign about rape prevention. In 2015, for instance, Sussex Police produced posters that advised women to stick together on nights out, to keep their friends safe.[17] Invariably these efforts invite a feminist backlash. Feminists typically argue that such campaigns imply that it's not the rapists themselves who are responsible, but the victims. The Sussex Police posters

Men and women are different

were met by a petition for their removal, with the feminist authors of the petition writing that 'the people who have the most power to prevent rape and sexual assault from happening are not friends or bystanders but rather the perpetrators of the crime – the rapists'.[18]

Which is true, of course it is! But here's the point: *rapists don't care what feminists have to say.* I sympathise with the feminist instinct to object to even the slightest suggestion of victim blaming, particularly by police, given that most police forces have a shameful history of blaming victims rather than the rapists, and there continue to be all sorts of problems with the criminal justice system. This is why I have spent most of my adult life campaigning to improve the system to ensure rapists are properly prosecuted. But posters that say 'don't rape' will prevent precisely zero rapes, because rape is already illegal, and would-be rapists know that. We can scream 'don't rape' until we're blue in the face, and it won't make a blind bit of difference.

It has to be possible to say simultaneously that rape is reprehensible, and also that it is ok – in fact, *essential* – to offer advice that could help to reduce its incidence. I could hardly have more contempt for rapists – I joke with my friends that I want to market a range of tiny guillotines to deal with rapists in a very direct manner – and yet I'm exhausted by feminists who can't move beyond just saying over and over again that rape is bad. Yes, rape is bad. We know that. Now let's actually do something about it.

There are two ways of reducing rape. The first is to constrain rapists, for instance by imprisoning them, and

Men and women are different

the second is to limit opportunities for them to act on their desires. Prosecution rates for sexual crimes are appallingly low in every part of the world – in the UK, less than one per cent of rapes result in a conviction. This is partly due to low reporting rates, partly due to failures within the criminal justice system, and partly due to the fact that it is inherently difficult to prosecute rape, given that it usually depends on the word of one person against another. It's always going to be challenging to prove beyond reasonable doubt the presence or absence of consent, even in a perfect system, and we don't have one of those.

I would like convicted rapists to spend much longer in prison – their whole lives, if needs be. The feminists who disagree with me present only one alternative to imprisonment: re-socialisation, typically attempted through consent workshops for children and young adults. I've both designed and taught these workshops and I don't think they're entirely useless. They can achieve two things: they can teach participants (including potential victims) what is and is not illegal, and they can offer schools or other institutions the opportunity to declare a zero-tolerance attitude. If, for instance, a student is caught sharing revenge porn having attended an official consent workshop, he or she can't plausibly claim not to have known that this was both illegal and punishable by expulsion.

However, consent workshops are very unlikely to prevent rape, because rape is not caused by a lack of education. Hundreds of thousands of years of sexual violence – not only in our own species, but also in many others – is not a

Men and women are different

consequence of some kind of misunderstanding. It cannot be swiftly cleared up during a forty-five-minute workshop in which kids are told in words of one syllable not to rape one another. In short: putting one's faith in re-socialisation is not only foolish, but dangerous.

If we accept the evidence from evolutionary biology and move beyond the standard feminist view, then we can understand that rapists are really just men who are aroused by violence, have poor impulse control, and are presented with a suitable victim and a suitable set of circumstances. Those circumstances can include: a victim who is drunk, high, or otherwise vulnerable, the absence of witnesses, and no fear of any legal or social repercussions. Both women and men in the sex trade are spectacularly vulnerable (much more on this in later chapters). And young women between the ages of about thirteen and twenty-five are the prime age group likely to be targeted.

If you wanted to design the perfect environment for the would-be rapist, then you couldn't do much better than a party or nightclub filled with young women who are wearing high heels (limiting mobility) and drinking or taking drugs (limiting awareness). Is it appalling for a person to even contemplate assaulting these women? Yes. Does that moral statement provide any protection to these women whatsoever? No. I made this mistake many, many times as a young woman, and I understand the pressure to conform. But, while young women should feel free to get hammered with their girlfriends or highly trusted men, doing so among strange men will always be risky.

Men and women are different

I think we all know this, just as we all know that it's risky for young women to hitchhike, travel alone, or go back to a strange man's house. The sorry truth is that an unknown minority of men pose a risk, and those men aren't always identifiable on first sight, or even when you know them well. So, my advice to young women has to be this: avoid putting yourself in a situation where you are alone with a man you don't know, or a man who gives you a bad feeling in your gut. He is almost certainly stronger and faster than you, which means that the only thing standing between you and rape is that man's self-control.

Other feminists can gnash their teeth all they like, accuse me of victim blaming, and insist that the burden should be on rapists, not their victims, to prevent rape. But they have no other solutions to offer, since feeble efforts at re-socialisation don't actually work. What does sometimes work is to (a) reduce the opportunities available to would-be rapists, and (b) to imprison those who either cannot or will not resist their aggressive sexual impulses. Because rape isn't only about power, it's also about sex.

NOT ALL DESIRES ARE GOOD

The American social psychologist Jonathan Haidt likes to invent scenarios that test our moral intuitions. He will ask people to listen to a story, give their opinion on it, and then explain their reasoning. Some of these scenarios are about sex. For instance, is it ok for a brother and sister to have sex, if they use multiple forms of contraception, and no one else knows about it? He has found that participants' responses tend to be affected by their politics. Social conservatives generally give swift, confident answers. For them, having sex with a sibling obviously violates religious or traditional moral rules and is therefore unacceptable. End of story.

Liberals have more difficulty: they want to say that incest, for instance, is wrong, because they are instinctively disgusted by it, but they struggle to give good reasons. If no one is directly being harmed, then where's the problem? Most therefore find themselves, in Haidt's words, 'dumbfounded'.

Not all desires are good

Not everyone is dumbfounded, however. A handful of radicals reject the idea of there being 'good' or 'bad' sexual behaviour, interpreting such moralising as inherently oppressive. To their minds, sex does not need to involve either love or commitment, and it certainly needn't have any connection to marriage or reproduction. The only thing that matters to these radicals is whether or not everyone involved is able and willing to consent to a particular sex act. All other sexual morality must be discarded.

This position is interpreted by its proponents as undermining traditional sexual norms. Such norms, they argue, historically made people with unusual sexual interests outcasts, or else made them permanently unhappy as they were forced to hide their desires. The idea that 'it is forbidden to forbid' (a slogan from student protests in the 1960s) has become remarkably mainstream since. It has become jumbled up with the feminist attempt to free women from traditional sexual restrictions that reduced their freedom and pleasure.

But I want to suggest that what is really going on is a class struggle. This is not a struggle between the revolutionaries and the traditionalists, but between two very different classes of people, with two very different sets of interests.

The sexual free market

'Sociosexuality' is the term that psychologists use to describe a person's interest in sexual variety. People with 'restricted sociosexuality' prefer monogamy (sexual relations with

Not all desires are good

only one mate over one period of time) and heavy emotional investment in long-term relationships. Those with 'unrestricted sociosexuality' like to have sex with as many people as possible, are quicker to have sex, and tend to be less emotionally invested in their romantic relationships.

In an enormous study across forty-eight countries, researchers found large differences between male and female sociosexuality everywhere.[1] There is of course variation within the sexes, with some individual women high in sociosexuality, and some individual men low in it. However, there is strong evidence to suggest that, on average, women are more motivated towards monogamy than men are.

This difference is explained by what evolutionary biologists term 'parental investment theory'. Women can produce offspring at a maximum rate of about one pregnancy per year. Promiscuous men, on the other hand, can theoretically produce offspring every time they orgasm. Although there are some exceptions, in general, natural selection has favoured women who are choosy about their mates.

We see this play out in male and female sexual behaviour. The research is clear. Men, on average, prefer to have more sex and with a larger number of partners. Sex buyers are almost exclusively male. Men watch a lot more porn than women do. The vast majority of women prefer a committed relationship to casual sex, if given the option.

In short, the evidence shows that sex acts that have become much more socially acceptable over the last sixty years are acts that men are much more likely to enjoy. It is a good time to be a sex buyer, a porn user, and a playboy. It is

Not all desires are good

the highly sociosexual who have done best out of the sexual revolution, and these people are overwhelmingly male.

There have also been other beneficiaries of sexual liberalisation. Lesbian, gay, and bisexual people have gained a lot. Their relationships are now not only decriminalised, but also granted state recognition in many countries. Homophobia in Western countries has fallen dramatically over the past one hundred years. In 1983, opinion polls suggested that about half of the public thought that 'sexual relations between adults of the same sex' were 'always wrong'.[2] By 2012, this proportion had more than halved. A year later, legislation introducing same-sex marriage in England and Wales was passed under a Conservative government. Since 2001, dozens of other countries have legalised same-sex marriage, including the United States in 2015.[3]

Any historical event as huge as the sexual revolution is going to have many effects, both good and bad. However, my key point is that it is wrong to see this as purely progress. Every social change involves gaining benefits that may not be compatible with other positive things. There are 'trade offs', where we must accept some drawbacks if we wish to gain some other advantages. This complexity is overlooked if we see change as being simply and only a good thing.

We have sex with other people. This means, of course, that the loving partner needs another loving partner. But this also means that the fetishist needs other people to participate in his fetish. The sex buyer needs sex sellers. The porn user needs porn producers. This isn't a problem for radical sexual liberals. They point out that plenty of people (mostly women) are available to provide for these desires – sometimes readily, sometimes in return for money. But this underestimates the extent to which such women may be forced to do so, if not by physical force then by other less obvious methods.

Chesterton's Fence

The term 'Chesterton's Fence' comes from the ideas of great Victorian writer G.K. Chesterton. He asks us to imagine walking down a country road and coming across a fence. The 'reformer', so says Chesterton, is likely to exclaim 'I don't see the use of this; let us clear it away.'[4] To which Chesterton responds that the person who doesn't understand the purpose of a fence is *the last person* who should be allowed to reform it. The question we must always ask ourselves is this: what function is the fence performing? What would we lose if we were to tear it down?

The world is big and complicated, and literally no one is capable of fully understanding it, or predicting how its systems might respond to change. But the sexual radicals do not recognise how complex sexual relationships really are. They cannot see that society is composed of both the strong and the vulnerable, as well as people who may play both roles at different times.

Their analysis can only understand people as separate, selfish individuals, looking for a good time. Thus, when they see a taboo – against, say, having sex with siblings – they assume that, if no obvious purpose for the taboo springs to

Not all desires are good

mind, it must therefore be unnecessary. They falsely assume that, with all such taboos removed, then we would all be capable of making entirely free and enjoyable choices about our sexual lives.

But, in fact, our choices are severely constrained. Firstly, because we are impressionable creatures who absorb the ideas and behaviour of others. Also, because sex is a social activity: it requires the involvement of other people.

If I am, for instance, a young female student looking for a boyfriend at my twenty-first-century university, and I don't want to have sex before marriage, then I will find my options limited in a way that they wouldn't have been seventy years ago. When sex before marriage is expected, and when almost all of the other women in my social group are willing to 'put out' on a first or second date, then *not* being willing to do the same becomes a competitive disadvantage.

There are two ways this student will find a boyfriend. The first is to be tremendously attractive, so that men will be prepared to wait to marry her to have sex with her. The other is to be happy to only date men who are as unusual as she is. Few women are tremendously attractive, and the second option severely limits her options. There are losers as well as winners from this change.

The wrong side of history

We tend to celebrate those historical figures credited with being ahead of their time and later vindicated. We venerate the people whose ideas won out, perhaps imagining

Not all desires are good

ourselves to be among their number. We think a lot less about the people who lost.

Campaigner Mary Whitehouse, who became famous in the 1960s, is one of history's losers. She spent thirty-seven years organising letter-writing campaigns aimed at stopping the increasing levels of sex and violence shown on British TV. She didn't campaign for change, she campaigned against it. And she failed utterly. Some of Whitehouse's concerns look rather silly now. She spent a long time campaigning against things that now appear very tame. For example, she protested against a suggestively placed microphone when rock star Mick Jagger appeared on popular music TV show *Top of the Pops* in the 1960s.

Whitehouse was very homophobic. She wrote articles in newspapers advising mothers on how to stop their sons becoming gay. She combined this homophobia with a campaign against blasphemy that often used very old-fashioned laws. In 1977, she prosecuted *Gay News* for printing a poem that described a Roman centurion fantasising about having sex with the body of the crucified Christ, and won. One of the lawyers in the case wrote that Whitehouse's 'fear of homosexuals was visceral' – he may well have been right.[5]

Her reputation as a ridiculous bigot means that if Whitehouse is remembered now, it is usually as a joke. She was constantly mocked even at the time. Indeed, some progressives now use Whitehouse's name as shorthand for being on the 'wrong side of history'.

However, this way of telling the story only works if one is deliberately selective. Whitehouse has found herself con-

Not all desires are good

demned by 'history' on the issues of homosexuality, blasphemy, and the phallic use of microphones on *Top of the Pops*. But Whitehouse was one of the few public figures of her day who gave a damn about child sexual abuse.

In the 1960s, 1970s and 1980s, the BBC was enabling mass sex abuse. The most famous example was TV presenter Jimmy Savile. It was only after Savile died, unpunished, in 2011 that the scale of his crimes became clear. It is now believed that, over the course of at least forty years, BBC staff turned a blind eye to the rape and sexual assault of up to one thousand girls and boys by Savile.[6] Savile's celebrity status enabled his sexual aggression, allowing him access to vulnerable victims, particularly children. His fame discouraged people from investigating him, even though Savile openly wrote about some of his criminal behaviour in his autobiography.

When the Savile scandal broke in the early 2010s, the same refrain was repeated by commentators again and again: 'it was a different time'.[7] And, indeed it was, although we sometimes forget quite how different attitudes towards child sexual abuse really were during the 1970s and 1980s. In Britain, an organisation calling itself the 'Paedophile Information Exchange' was openly campaigning to legalise sex with children. They found themselves welcomed warmly by some politicians. Margaret Thatcher's government refused demands to ban the group.[8]

In the United States, NAMBLA (the 'North American Man/Boy Love Association') was founded at the end of the 1970s, and attracted support from some very famous

Not all desires are good

people.[9] In 1977, a petition to the French parliament calling for the decriminalisation of sex between adults and children was signed by a long list of famous philosophers and other thinkers. In some European countries at this time, such as Sweden, child pornography was freely available and even legal.[10]

All of these shocking things now seem on 'the wrong side of history', since the 1990s saw a sharp swing back against efforts to normalise paedophilia. During the 1970s it was primarily 'backwards' conservatives who opposed groups like the Paedophile Information Exchange. Mary Whitehouse, for instance, lobbied hard for a law to protect children from abuse. Eventually, Whitehouse was joined by progressives in her condemnation of child sexual abuse, but her contribution was erased. The shameful history of liberal tolerance for paedophilia in the decades following the sexual revolution was mostly forgotten.

Paedophilia is now condemned by liberals and conservatives alike. For liberals the problem with paedophilia is that children can't consent, and therefore any sexual activity involving them will always be unacceptable. They claimed that pro-paedophilia campaigns in the 1970s were unfortunate blips on a general path towards progress.

Upon closer scrutiny, the consent argument falls apart. Liberals may be able to accept the banning of child porn, since it necessitates the abuse of real children in its production. However, what about images that the police term 'pseudo-photographs', that appear to depict real children? What about illustrations? What about adults dressing up

Not all desires are good

and pretending to be children during sex? What about porn performers who appear to be very young? What about porn performers who deliberately make themselves look even younger? Who dress up to look like children? Doesn't that instinctively seem wrong?

But how can liberals condemn such things? An ethical system based solely on consent does not allow space for this kind of moral instinct.

Breaking taboos

When you set out to break down sexual taboos, you shouldn't be surprised when *all* taboos are considered fair game for breaking, including the ones you'd rather keep.

Progressives in the 1970s who wanted to legalise sex with children never said that consent was unimportant. They simply claimed that, because children develop at different rates, some children may be able to meaningfully consent to sex. They also pointed out, correctly, that paedophiles are a maligned sexual minority who suffer greatly as a result of the taboo maintained against them. These arguments are perfectly in line with the sorts of argument used to justify the sexual revolution. The principles of sexual liberalism do, I'm sorry to say, inevitably tend towards legalising child sex, whether or not we want them to.

And, indeed, we are now starting to see some slippage back towards the thinking of the 1970s. In 2020, Netflix released a film called *Cuties* (originally *Mignonnes*). The main character is eleven-year-old Amy, who lives with her

Not all desires are good

Senegalese family in a poor district of Paris. When Amy's father announces his intention to take a second wife, Amy and her mother are heartbroken, and the rupture pushes Amy away from her conservative religious community. She joins a group of girls who call themselves the 'Cuties'.

The Cuties are not nice girls. They bully Amy and each other, they physically attack other children, they steal, they lie, and they also twerk. Aged eleven, they have formed an amateur dance troupe and adopted skimpy outfits. The girls aren't directly groomed by anyone and, in fact, we never see any overt acts of sexual aggression. They learn to grind and pout via the internet, particularly social media. Amy teaches the other girls to add more explicit moves to their routine and, in one explicit scene, the children encourage each other to jiggle their tiny backsides and hump the floor in an imitation of porn.

The film became very controversial and there was a social media storm. Some American politicians demanded that Netflix executives face a criminal investigation for the 'distribution of child pornography'.[11] Netflix defended the film by pointing out that it was intended as a commentary on the harms of child sexualisation. The problem was that it also featured a lot of *actual* child sexualisation. The adverts for the film exploited this, featuring photos of the four very young actresses dressed in glorified bikinis and arranged in suggestive poses.

Nevertheless, *Cuties* received positive reviews in many leading newspapers. One reviewer praised the film as a response to 'an age terrified of child sexuality' and later

Not all desires are good

tweeted his delight that the film had 'pissed off all the right people'.[12] These reviews suggested that outrage over the film was an hysterical overreaction caused by ridiculous conservative fear-mongering.

It is becoming fashionable among snobbish progressives to present anti-paedophilia anxiety as an obsession of the 'stupid' working classes, a group very much considered to be on 'the wrong side of history'. And yet there have been many shocking examples of child sexual abuse taking place at scale and without detection. Jimmy Savile abusing up to a thousand children on BBC premises would sound like a conspiracy theory if we didn't know it to be true.

The virtue of repression

In an episode of *The Simpsons* called 'I Am Furious (Yellow)', first aired in 2002, Homer Simpson decides to become a less angry person. Every time Homer finds himself feeling angry, he represses the emotion, and a lump appears on his neck. Soon enough, Homer's neck is covered in lumps and his calm demeanour is becoming increasingly fragile. At the end of the episode, Bart and Millhouse play a prank on Homer and all of this repressed anger is suddenly released in an uncontrolled rampage. Later in hospital, the doctor informs the Simpson family that Homer's attempts at emotional repression could have proved lethal since, without the opportunity for release, 'the anger would've overwhelmed his nervous system'. Repression, it seems, is not only difficult, but also dangerous.

Not all desires are good

It is common nowadays to understand sexual psychology in the following way. Sexual desire is seen to be a fixed quantity, which must be periodically released, either through actual sex or through some other kind of 'safety valve', like porn. If it is not released – if it is 'repressed' – there will be a dangerous build up.

The problem with this idea is that it does not recognise the necessity of sexual repression. Even now, after sexual attitudes have relaxed a lot, the law often requires us to repress our sexual impulses. If you want to have sex with someone, but they do not consent, then the law obliges you to repress your desire. You are also forbidden from having sex with an animal, and you may risk imprisonment if you masturbate or have sex in a public place. Every society requires that some kinds of sexual impulse be repressed – what varies is where exactly the line is drawn.

The word 'Victorian' is often used in association with sexual repression, as the Victorian era is a relatively recent example of a swing towards prudish attitudes. There is no doubt that the Victorians were more sexually repressive than we are nowadays, and that this resulted in terrible cruelties, primarily against gay men and unmarried mothers. Sexual repression is a blunt instrument, but it is not one we can do away with altogether, as the errors of the 1970s show. The radical desires of sexual liberals do not work in a world in which human sexuality is not always beautiful, but often wicked and repulsive. The desire to free the weak is a good one, but reckless action can also result in freedom for the powerful to prey on the weak.

Not all desires are good

The progressive story disguises this truth and, in doing so, does terrible harm to the more vulnerable. A society that prioritises the desires of the highly sociosexual is necessarily one that prioritises the desires of men, given the natural distribution of this trait. Those men then need to call on other people – mostly young women – to satisfy their desires.

The sexual radicals will dismiss this problem by insisting that these young women are perfectly capable of freely saying 'no'. They might even suggest that I am being patronising in suggesting otherwise. But attempts at exercising one's free will in the face of sexual coercion do not always work out well: you may know of some examples yourself.

It is a bit like when people are taken advantage of at work. In theory they can refuse requests from their boss to work overtime, but they know they are less likely to get promoted if they do. Their boss has the power to help or hinder their career. There is not a level playing field. The sexual playing field is not level either, but it suits the interests of the powerful to pretend that it is.

When we strip back all sexual morality to the bare bones, leaving only the principle of consent, we leave the way clear for predators. As the example of paedophilia advocacy shows, making consent the only relevant moral principle is not strong enough to protect the vulnerable from harm. Given the profound importance and complexity of sexual relationships, a much more sophisticated moral system is required.

Reverting to traditionalism doesn't solve the problem. Although I reject the chronological snobbery of

Not all desires are good

progressivism that dismisses the dead as stupid and malevolent, the world we live in now is very different from the world in which ancient religious ethics were formulated. Our ancestors were confronted with realities that are wildly different from our own. They had no reliable contraception, lived in smaller and less complex societies, experienced very high birth and death rates, and so on. Exactly imitating the past cannot teach us how to live in the twenty-first century.

Appealing to moral intuition takes us some of the way. Sexual liberalism asks us to train ourselves out of the kind of instinctive revulsion that often has a protective function. This is well illustrated by the example of the American actor Armie Hammer. Various of Armie Hammer's exes have accused him of having violent and degrading sexual tastes. They have claimed that he enjoyed inflicting pain on them during sex and that he also spoke about his desire to break their bones, eat their skin, and barbecue their flesh.[13]

You'd think this might have been a red flag. And yet the women who had sexual relationships with Hammer seem to have accepted the liberal view that we should ignore our moral instinct of disgust. So, while they didn't exactly *like* Hammer's interest in cannibalism, they didn't feel able to object to it either. This meant that they were pulled into the orbit of a dangerous and abusive man.

Sexual liberalism is misguided not only in disregarding, but in *actively resisting* moral intuition. And yet, at the same time, much like the principle of consent, intuition is too simplistic to be serviceable on its own. We may be able to agree broadly on the most outrageous examples (cannibal-

Not all desires are good

ism, say), but one person's gut instinct won't always be the same as another person's.

I can't pretend that this is an easy issue to resolve, because 'how should we behave sexually?' is really just another way of asking 'how should we behave?' and, after millennia of effort, we are nowhere near reaching an agreement on the answer to that question.

Nevertheless, here is my attempt at a contribution: we should treat our sexual partners with dignity. We should not regard other people as merely body parts to be enjoyed. We should aspire to love and mutuality in all of our sexual relationships, regardless of whether they are gay or straight. We should prioritise virtue over desire. We should not assume that any given feeling we discover in our hearts (or our loins) ought to be acted upon.

Armie Hammer should have repressed his desire to hurt his sexual partners and Jimmy Savile should have repressed his desire to sexually violate children. Doing so would have done them no harm, because some degree of sexual repression is good and necessary. The world would be a better place if such men were more ashamed of their desires, and acted on that shame by mastering themselves. But it's not only the most appalling abusers who could do with putting virtue before desire. All of us are likely to be tempted by our worst instincts every now and again, and we are much more likely to indulge them in a culture that encourages us to.

Actor Aziz Ansari, like Armie Hammer, was involved in a recent sex scandal, although his behaviour was less obviously

Not all desires are good

bad. In 2017, Ansari went on a date with a woman publicly known only as 'Grace'. They went back to his house, and then had some sexual contact that left Grace feeling deeply uncomfortable. Although she gently pulled away, mumbling her reluctance, Ansari tried again and again to initiate sex. Eventually, at his request, she gave him a blow job. He never used any force, and she never actually said 'no', but Grace was left feeling used. The next day, she texted Ansari telling him as much and he apologised for having 'misread things'. Several months later, she published her account on the website *babe*.[14]

Ansari's behaviour did not meet the legal threshold for rape because Grace did technically consent to their encounter. Ansari clearly assumed that Grace would want to have sex with him – both because of his celebrity status, and because having sex after a first date is now the norm among young, 'sexually liberated' Westerners. And Grace was therefore put in a position in which she had to make the case *against* their having sex, and she found it almost impossible to do so. She instinctively wanted to defend her sexual boundaries, but she was thwarted by a culture in which 'it's just sex' is the dominant view. They were two consenting adults who had just been on a date, and sex was the expected way to end the night, so how could she say 'no'?

Following the publication of Grace's account, liberal feminist commentators tried to condemn Ansari within the consent framework, suggesting that in fact that encounter hadn't been truly consensual, against the available evidence. Given that the need for consent is the only moral principle

Not all desires are good

left for sexual liberals, they had to do so. The problem is that the presence of consent is such a very, very low bar. Ansari had managed to jump this bar, but he had also failed to behave well.

A sophisticated system of sexual ethics needs to demand more of people and, as the stronger and hornier sex, men must demonstrate even greater restraint than women. The word 'chivalry' is now deeply unfashionable, but it describes something of what I'm calling for. In the coming chapters, I'll explore some of the self-interested reasons why men might choose chivalry. But the motivation to act decently ought to go beyond self-interest. It isn't against the law to cheat on a partner, or to accept sexual favours from a person you don't respect, or to very subtly coerce someone into sex, but it is isn't decent either. There are a lot of sexual behaviours that are neither criminal nor good. Somewhere between sexual liberalism and traditionalism, it has to be possible to find a better way.

LOVELESS SEX IS NOT EMPOWERING

In the first-ever episode of popular 1990s TV show *Sex and the City*, one of the main characters, Carrie Bradshaw, resolves to stop looking for 'Mr Perfect' and start enjoying herself. In that effort, she hooks up with an ex-boyfriend, 'a self-centred, withholding creep' to whom she no longer has any emotional attachment. She drops round at his place mid-afternoon, enjoys his offer of oral sex, and then leaves before he's had a chance to orgasm himself. Ignoring his irritation, Carrie tells us of her delight:

> As I began to get dressed, I realised that I'd done it. I'd just had sex like a man. I left feeling powerful, potent and incredibly alive. I felt like I owned this city. Nothing and no one could get in my way.

This example tells us something important about how female sexual liberation is seen. Carrie Bradshaw demon-

Loveless sex is not empowering

strates her sexual freedom by having loveless sex with a man she doesn't like. She shows no regard for his emotions and discards him immediately afterwards. The purpose of the encounter is physical gratification and asserting psychological dominance. Thus, it seems that what the phrase having sex 'like a man' really means is having sex *like an arsehole.*

Nevertheless, liberal feminism understands having sex 'like a man' as the obvious way for women to free themselves from old-fashioned expectations. If you believe that there is nothing wrong with treating other people as objects in pursuit of your own sexual satisfaction, then this makes sense. And if you believe that men and women are both physically and psychologically much the same, save for a few hang-ups absorbed from a sex negative culture, then why wouldn't you want women to do so?

The sex writer and TV producer Karley Sciortino is a particularly enthusiastic proponent of this view. To her mind, the sexual double standard – by which male promiscuity is viewed as neutral or positive, while female promiscuity is frowned upon – is the product of an oppressively anti-sex society. The solution, as she sees it, is to train ourselves out of negative responses to what she would call 'sluttiness':

Today we've created an environment where (allegedly predatory) male sexuality needs to be policed, and (allegedly passive) female sexuality needs to be protected . . . It's outdated, it's offensive, and it's psychologically destructive for women, because it has the power to mislead girls into thinking that having

Loveless sex is not empowering

one not-ideal sexual experience means that they have lost part of themselves. *Hello* – pitying and victimising women doesn't help us: it just dismisses the importance of female sexual agency.[1]

The ambiguous words 'not-ideal' are doing a lot of work here, because Sciortino does acknowledge that the playing field is not entirely even. For one thing, there is the difference in physical strength that means that any heterosexual encounter will inevitably be more dangerous for the woman. For another, there is the risk of pregnancy.

But the liberal feminist argument leads us to conclude that you *must* 'have sex like a man' if you want to be a good feminist, and mostly it will turn out ok, and when it doesn't? When a sexual encounter turns out to be 'not-ideal', or worse? Well then, we must fall back on liberal feminism's old standby: 'teach men not to rape'.

The problem with this position is that we cannot just pretend that the world is safe, and that the existence of 'predatory male sexuality' is no more than an outdated stereotype. As we saw in Chapter 2, sexual violence in the real world actually follows the stereotype very closely – it really is men who rape, and it really is young women who are most at risk. This isn't a reality we can just ignore.

The sociosexuality gap

Men and women are not the same, either physically or psychologically. Casual heterosexual sex inherently carries

Loveless sex is not empowering

much greater risks for women, and in return for much smaller rewards. And yet the (perfectly reasonable) insistence that women should be *allowed* to 'have sex like a man' slips all too easily towards the insistence that they therefore *ought to*.

Carrie Bradshaw is, crucially, an aspirational character: attractive, glamorous, and professionally successful. Her model is one that we are supposed to follow, and Sciortino encourages her readers to do so. I don't doubt that there are some women who genuinely enjoy casual sex and who decide, having weighed the risks and benefits, that it is in their best interests to do so. What I question is the claim that *a culture of casual sex* is somehow of benefit to women in general.

I've written earlier in this book about what psychologists term 'sociosexuality' – the trait that determines a person's interest in sexual variety and adventure. The standard questionnaire used by researchers to assess sociosexuality asks respondents questions such as:[2]

- With how many different partners have you had sex within the past twelve months?
- With how many different partners have you had sexual intercourse without having an interest in a long-term committed relationship with this person?
- Do you agree that sex without love is OK?
- Do you only want to have sex with a person when you are sure that you will have a long-term, serious relationship?

Loveless sex is not empowering

Worldwide, there is a significant difference in average socio-sexuality between the sexes, with men generally much keener to sow their wild oats than women are. And there is a compelling evolutionary explanation for this difference, as we saw in Chapter 2.[3]

Although it's typical for men to invest a great deal of time and energy into children produced within marriage, men also have an alternative mode of sexuality. They can favour quantity of offspring over quality – that is, inseminate as many women as possible and not hang around to deal with the consequences. This alternative is favoured more by some individual men than others, depending on their degree of sociosexuality, but the difference is not absolute. Some men may be drawn more towards one sexual strategy than the other at certain points in their lives, or in certain situations, or with certain partners.

Nonetheless, when they are given a choice, women are generally much pickier than men and reject a much larger proportion of suitors. For instance, one study from 1978 – since repeated, with exactly the same findings – involved participants of average attractiveness approaching strangers of a similar age and propositioning them for sex.[4] As the authors write:

> The great majority of men were willing to have a sexual liaison with the women who approach them. Not one woman agreed to a sexual liaison.

Some feminists would attribute this to a sex negative culture in which women suffer greater reputational damage

Loveless sex is not empowering

when they are seen as being too promiscuous. However, this explanation cannot account for the fact that women are also much pickier on dating apps and websites than men are, and that men and women also differ dramatically in their baseline levels of sexual disgust.[5] Disgust induces a physiological response that can be measured through heart and respiration rate, blood pressure, and salivation, although the individual may not be aware of these indicators.[6] Studies find that, on average, the sexual disgust threshold is much lower for women than it is for men.

Curiously, I am not aware of any word in the English language for an emotion that every woman I've spoken to has experienced at least once, but that the men I've spoken to don't seem to recognise at all. It is a combination of both sexual disgust and fear – the bone-deep, nauseating feeling of being trapped in proximity to a horny man who repulses you. This emotion can be provoked by being groped in a crowd, or leered at while travelling alone, or propositioned a little too forcefully in a bar. It is an emotion that women in the sex industry are forced to repress. In fact, as the prostitution survivor Rachel Moran has written, the ability not to cry or vomit in response to sexual fear and disgust is one of the essential 'skills' demanded by the industry.[7]

More than any other area of life, prostitution reveals the sometimes vast differences between male and female sexual behaviour. Women make up the overwhelmingly majority of sex sellers, for the simple reason that almost all sex buyers are male (at least 99 per cent in every part of the world) and most men are straight.

Loveless sex is not empowering

Sex buyers, by definition, are people who seek out sex outside of a committed relationship, usually with a person they have never met before. This kind of sexual encounter is far, far more likely to appeal to people high in sociosexuality. People low in this trait *are just not interested* in having sex with a stranger. The people exceptionally high in sociosexuality are overwhelmingly men, and the people exceptionally low in it are overwhelmingly women. This means that, as a rule, any sexual culture that encourages women to 'have sex like a man' will just encourage many women to have sex in a way that makes them miserable.

A hand held in daylight

The heterosexual dating market has a problem, and it's not one that can be easily resolved. Male sexuality and female sexuality, at the population level, do not match. On average, men want casual sex more often than women do, and women want committed monogamy more often than men do. Hook-up culture demands that women suppress their natural instincts in order to match male sexuality and thus meet the male demand for no-strings sex. Some women are quite happy to do this, but most women find it unpleasant, or even distressing. Thus hook-up culture is a solution to the sexuality mismatch that benefits some men, at the expense of most women.

I propose a different solution, based on a fundamental feminist claim: unwanted sex is worse than sexual frustration. I'm not willing to accept a sexual culture that puts

Loveless sex is not empowering

pressure on people low in sociosexuality (overwhelmingly women) to meet the sexual demands of those high in sociosexuality (overwhelmingly men). This is particularly unfair, given that sex carries so many more risks for women, in terms of violence and pregnancy. Hook-up culture is a terrible deal for women, and yet has been presented by liberal feminism as a form of liberation. A truly feminist project would demand that, in the straight dating world, it should be men, not women, who adjust their sexual appetites.

This argument is a long way from the feminist mainstream in the twenty-first century. Progressive media outlets churn out articles with headlines like '5 Fantastic Ways to Engage in Feminist Hookup Culture', which argue that, with consent, anything goes.[8] But this approach overstates the extent to which any of us can make truly free choices in a system in which we are all radically restricted and there is no level playing field. And it leaves no space for the sociosexuality gap – after all, how could it? Liberal feminism can hardly bear to recognise the existence of *physical* differences between the sexes, let alone psychological ones.

In a darkly funny article published in 2020, *Elle* magazine wrestled with some of the problems thrown up by hook-up culture, but without acknowledging the basic problem.[9] Rather than recognise the sexual differences between men and women, the writers instead attempt to carve out a new category, 'demisexuals'. They defined it as 'a select few members of society', who just aren't enthused about casual sex:

Loveless sex is not empowering

Struggling to identify with her sexuality for years, in 2016 *Washington Post* writer Meryl Williams detailed how she came across the term 'demisexuality' on Twitter and started an investigation into what it meant, which ultimately helped her come to terms with her own sexual orientation. 'I'm just glad that a term for my sexuality exists, even if it's one I'll probably have to explain to my future partners', she wrote.

What Williams is actually describing here is typical female sexuality. She isn't special, she's a normal woman who has just enough emotional insight to recognise that hook-up culture isn't good for her, but is lacking the political insight to recognise the existence of a bigger problem.

A more depressing type of pop-feminist article comes at the sociosexuality gap from a different angle. Such articles advise women to try to overcome their perfectly normal and healthy preference for intimacy and commitment in sexual relationships. They have titles like 'How to Bio-Hack Your Brain to Have Sex Without Getting Emotionally Attached'. They advise readers, for instance, to avoid making eye contact with their partners during sex, in an effort to avoid 'making an intimate connection'.[10] Readers are also advised to avoid alcohol, since for women (but, tellingly, not men) this seems to increase 'the likelihood they will bond prematurely'.

These guides are all carefully phrased to present the problem as gender-neutral, but the research on male and female sexuality makes clear what is really happening here.

Loveless sex is not empowering

Overwhelmingly *women* are being advised to cripple themselves emotionally in order to gratify men.

In the West, hook-up culture is now the normal expectation among young adults. Both popular culture and survey data indicate that sexual behaviour outside of traditional committed romantic relationships has become increasingly socially acceptable.[11] And, although it is possible for young women to opt out, research suggests that only a minority do so.[12] Absent some kind of religious commitment, this is now the 'normal' route presented to girls as they become sexually active. And young people tend to be *very anxious* about being 'normal'.

Leah Fessler has written thoughtfully about her time as a student at Middlebury College. This was a college where hook-up culture reigned, and abstinence seemed to be the only way in which a female student could avoid participating.[13] Unwilling to commit to celibacy, Fessler convinced herself that emotionless sex was the feminist thing to do, and she did her best to ignore her unhappiness:

> After I began having sex with these guys, the power balance always tipped. A few hookups in, I'd begin to obsess, primarily about the ambiguity of it all. My friends and I would analyze incessantly: Does he like me? Do you like him? He hasn't texted in a day. Read this text. I'm so confused. He said he didn't want anything, but keeps asking to hang out . . . With time, inevitably, came attachment. And with attachment came shame, anxiety, and emptiness.

Loveless sex is not empowering

The worst thing for women at Middlebury were the 'pseudo-relationships':

> . . . . The mutant children of meaningless sex and loving partnerships. Two students consistently hook-up with one another – and typically, only each other – for weeks, months, even years. Yet per unspoken social code, neither party is permitted emotional involvement, commitment, or vulnerability. To call them exclusive would be 'clingy', or even 'crazy'.

Fessler and her friends quietly admitted to each other that what they really wanted was true intimacy: public recognition of a relationship, an arm around the waist, 'a hand held in daylight'. She wrote her senior-year thesis on hook-up culture at Middlebury. Of the straight women who participated in her research, the vast majority stated a clear preference for committed relationships. Only eight per cent of women who said they were presently in pseudo-relationships reported being 'happy' with their situation. Other studies consistently find the same thing: following hook-ups, women are more likely than men to experience regret, low self-esteem, and mental distress.[14] And, most of the time, they don't even orgasm.

Female pleasure is rare during casual sex. Men in casual relationships are just not as good at bringing women to orgasm, compared with men in committed relationships. In first time hook-ups, only ten per cent of women orgasm,

Loveless sex is not empowering

compared to 68 per cent of women in long-term relationships.[15] The evidence doesn't reveal a generation of women revelling in sexual liberation – instead, a lot of women seem to be having unpleasant, crappy sex out of a sense of obligation.

But the liberal feminist narrative of sexual empowerment is popular for a reason: it is much more palatable to understand oneself as a sassy, empowered Carrie Bradshaw. Adopting such a self-image can be protective, making it easier to endure what is often, in fact, a rather miserable experience. If you're a young woman launched into a sexual culture that is fundamentally not geared towards protecting your safety or wellbeing, and if your only options seem to be either hooking up or strict celibacy, then a comforting myth of 'agency' can be attractive.

This myth depends on naivety about the true nature of male sexuality. Today's young women are typically unaware that men are, in general, much better suited to emotionless sex, and find it much easier to regard their sexual partners as disposable. Ignorant of this fact, women can all too easily fail to recognise that being desired is not at all the same thing as being held in high esteem.

It isn't nice to think of oneself as disposable, nor to acknowledge that other people view you that way. Often, it's easier to turn away from any acknowledgement of what is really going on, at least temporarily. I've spoken to a lot of women who participated in hook-up culture when they were young, and only years later came to realise just how unhappy it made them. I've yet to meet anyone who has

Loveless sex is not empowering

travelled the same emotional journey, but in the opposite direction.

Cads and dads

While most women assess their short-term and their long-term partners based on the same criteria, most men do not.[16] A woman will typically look for identical qualities in a hook-up as she does in a husband. As the evolutionary psychologist David Buss puts it, 'in both cases, women want someone who is kind, romantic, understanding, exciting, stable, healthy, humorous, and generous with his resources. In both contexts, women desire men who are tall, athletic, and attractive.'[17] Men, in contrast, tend to be very particular about what they look for in a potential wife (when they are in 'dad' mode), but much less so when seeking out casual sex (when they are in 'cad' mode).

Sherry Argov, bestselling dating advice author, puts it frankly:

> What men don't want women to know is that, almost immediately, they put women into one of two categories: 'good time only' or 'worthwhile'. And the minute he slides you into that 'good time only' category, you'll almost never come back out.[18]

There is a straightforward scientific reason for the existence of these two categories: it is hard to dissuade men from their instinct to care about what evolutionary biologists call

Loveless sex is not empowering

'paternity certainty' (knowing for sure that they are the biological father of the children that they help bring up). Men in 'cad' mode aren't concerned with the welfare of their unknown offspring, since they are favouring quantity over quality, but men in 'dad' mode care a great deal, and will often devote their lives to providing for their families.

But 'dad' mode carries a significant cost. In our evolutionary history, men who unwittingly devoted themselves to raising children not genetically related to them were at risk of helping someone else's genes be passed on. On the other hand, those who practised what biologists call 'mate guarding' – i.e. behaving jealously – could be certain that their children were their own. The sexual double standard is the result of this mate guarding instinct.

Like all other features of our evolutionary past, there is room for flexibility here. Plenty of men (and women) are utterly devoted to their adoptive or step-children, regardless of their genetic link. However, in general the sexual double standard is so prevalent and so fiercely held that it is considered by some who study the diversity of human societies to be present in all of them.[19]

Although it may no longer be acknowledged, the sexual double standard does persist. For adolescents, the association between lifetime number of sexual partners and social status varies significantly by sex. Boys who sleep with more people have greater social status, but girls who do the same have lower status.[20] Among adults, promiscuity in men is generally viewed neutrally, whereas a woman's reputation is damaged as her number of sexual partners increases.[21]

Loveless sex is not empowering

People may be reluctant to actually say so outright, but privately there is a social penalty suffered by women viewed as promiscuous.

When looking for a long-term partner, anonymous surveys suggest that the vast majority of straight men prefer to choose a wife with a limited sexual history and little interest in casual sex. Women also prefer a husband who is not unusually promiscuous, but their preference is not as strong. Most are willing to accept a man who has historically enjoyed casual sex but has since settled down.[22]

Importantly, however, men generally don't mind a more extensive sexual history when they're looking for a hook-up. Then, in fact, promiscuity may increase the appeal. With a high sexual disgust threshold, a natural interest in sexual variety, no personal risk of pregnancy, and no fear of slut shaming, casual sex presents few risks to men. And the liberal feminist narrative of 'having sex like a man' provides comfort for any man whose conscience might trouble him.

With hook-up culture established as normative, both men and women are funnelled into patterns of behaviour that are grimly complementary. Men are encouraged into 'cad' mode. They pursue temporary relationships that offer all of the pleasures of cheap sex and none of the responsibilities of commitment. Meanwhile, women compete with each other for short-term male sexual attention, and may well win it, but in a form liable to induce (in Leah Fessler's words) 'shame, anxiety, and emptiness'.

Loveless sex is not empowering

Mutual incomprehension

Just like their female peers, men may not consciously realise that this is what they're participating in. And, in one sense, who can blame them? Teenage boys are raised on pop culture that presents having sex 'like a man' as the ultimate form of female sexual empowerment. In the porn they are typically exposed to from childhood, women are shown *begging* men for painful or degrading sex acts. When young men start having sex offline, they will likely encounter women – themselves schooled by porn and pop culture – who hide their distress, fake their orgasms, and work hard to avoid 'catching feelings'.

We should hardly be surprised when, after all this, many men assume that women *really don't mind* being relegated to 'good time only'. The resulting dysfunction can be glimpsed in posts like this, on the r/relationships subreddit:

I was hanging out with my friends with benefits on Thursday after work. We been hooking up for six months. I was heating us up some food and she started asking about what I look for in a long-term girlfriend.

I told her that I want someone successful, and someone that I think would make a good mom. She starts then talking about how she has those qualities and I see how this conversation is going so I change the topic.

She brings it up and starts asking me what should she focus on to be the kind of girl guys want to marry

Loveless sex is not empowering

one day. I told her she is fine the way she is, she just needs to find the right guy. She asked me why I don't want to date her down the road when I am looking for something.

I told her, that she is great, but she isn't really girlfriend material in my eyes. She started crying like crazy after that. I don't know what was going on we never had a thing, she never talked about having feelings or anything.[23]

This man seems to be genuinely bewildered by the fact that the woman he has been having sex with for many months is unhappy. And the woman seems to have drifted into this arrangement, not realising how little regard her partner really has for her. This is a tragedy of mutual incomprehension.

A casual sex culture disproportionately benefits men. But that isn't to say that there isn't an eventual cost to be borne by the men. A man in his twenties with a different partner every week might have a certain glamour, but no man in his sixties or seventies can sustain that. Even if he were still able to attract casual partners (a big 'if'), his peers would regard him as a dirty old man. Casual sex harms men too, though not as immediately, and not as obviously.

But casual sex harms women most of all. I realise that avoiding it will often be difficult, given the pressures that young women face now. Nonetheless, unless you are in the small minority of highly sociosexual women, the risks of casual sex will outweigh the benefits.

Loveless sex is not empowering

Being alone with an unknown, horny man will always be somewhat dangerous for any woman, given the differences in size and strength. And, although it's of course true that husbands and long-term boyfriends also commit domestic violence, that's no reason to do away with the vetting process altogether. It's better to date men that are already part of one's social network. If they've developed a reputation for treating their girlfriends badly, you are likely to hear about this through mutual friends. When you date a stranger from the internet, the only person who can give you information about his sexual history is the man himself, and his account is often unreliable. What's more, there is nothing stopping him from treating his date badly and then melting back into the night, having suffered no social consequences whatsoever. Mutual friends and acquaintances can punish bad behaviour. Dating apps can't.

The fact that a man wants to have sex with a woman *is not an indication* that he wants a relationship with her. Holding off on having sex for at least the first few months is therefore a good strategy for several reasons. Firstly, it filters out the men who are just looking for a hook-up. Secondly, it gives a woman time to get to know a man before putting herself in a position of vulnerability. Thirdly, avoiding the emotional attachment that comes with a sexual relationship makes it easier to spot red flags. Free from the befuddling effects of hormones, it's possible to assess a new boyfriend's behaviour with clearer eyes.

One of the factors that acts against women in heterosexual dating is the gender gap in the personality trait that

Loveless sex is not empowering

psychologists call 'agreeableness' – in other words, 'niceness'. It has long been known by researchers that, on average, women are much more agreeable than men.[24]

Agreeable people are more likely to put their own interests last, and more likely to think the best of people, against the evidence. I'm a very agreeable person, which means, for instance, that I tend to avoid interpersonal conflict and I'm terrible at negotiating pay. If you want to know how agreeable you are, you can search online for 'big five personality test'. It's a useful thing to know about yourself, because it can help to guide your behaviour. Because I am naturally agreeable, I make a conscious effort to be more assertive. Agreeable people are particularly vulnerable to being taken advantage of by disagreeable people. Given that women are on average significantly more agreeable than men are, this has obvious relevance to sexual politics.

So, my advice to agreeable women assessing potential partners is not to ask yourself 'would this man make a good boyfriend *for me?*' Doing so risks allowing your niceness to override your good sense. Ask yourself instead 'would this man make a good *father to my children?*' Not because you necessarily intend to have children with this man, but because agreeable people find it easier to prioritise the interests of people they love than to prioritise their own interests. And if he wouldn't make a good father, don't have sex with him. It means that he isn't worthy of your trust.

Liberal feminism prizes having sex 'like a man' as a route to women's liberation. But we will never be able to have sex like men, because we will never be men, despite modern

Loveless sex is not empowering

contraception and other technology giving us the illusion of sameness. We can either accept that fact, and act accordingly, or we can maintain our current illusions, which just results in lots of young women getting badly hurt.

I'd also like to live in a world in which women can do whatever they want, without fear of what men might do to them. But we don't live in that world. So we have to accept, and adapt to, reality.

CONSENT IS NOT ENOUGH

This chapter is about the predatory nature of the porn industry and its destructive effects on the people involved in it. The only defence that the porn industry has, when presented with its hideous list of crimes, is its own version of the progressive sexual liberation story. Everyone is consenting, everyone is an adult, the women like it, and *who are you to say otherwise?*

Now, we might respond by pointing out that actually not everyone *is* an adult, and not everyone *is* consenting. This is because many images of child rape can be found even on the most mainstream porn platforms. But the industry and its defenders are quick to dismiss such examples as exceptions. They argue that so long as the porn 'actresses' are old enough, (moderately) sane enough, and don't say 'no' at the crucial moment, then when they reach the age of consent, anything goes.

Consent is not enough

For practical reasons, the age of consent has to serve as a legal bright line. It separates what is called statutory rape (sex that is rape by definition because it is with a child, who is deemed to be unable to consent in law) from consensual sex. It is true that young people mature at different rates, and the transition from childhood to adulthood is, like night turning to day, a gradual process. Nonetheless, we have to establish some clear marker. At 11pm, she is a child; at midnight, she becomes an adult. That's how it has to be.

But consent has more layers to it than that. There is the barest definition of the term that we have to rely on in a court of law: did she and could she say 'no'? But there is also a deeper meaning. And here I'm afraid we're going to have to let go of simple ideas about consent. Although 'but she consented' may do as a legal defence, it is not a convincing *moral* defence.

Grooming

The grim truth is that people – particularly young women – will sometimes claim that they consented to some of the worst harms you can imagine.

In recent decades, a set of gangs of men sexually abused victims in dozens of British cities across the UK. The victims of these 'grooming gangs' have mainly been teenage girls, particularly those from poor and troubled families, many of whom were brought up in care.

Although some of these victims do desperately seek out help, only to be turned away, it is far more common for girls

Consent is not enough

to reject anyone who tries to help. Sometimes they do this because they've been intimidated into silence. More often it's because of something very troubling. They think that the adult men abusing them are their loving boyfriends.

This is what is meant by the term 'grooming'. It means brainwashing, or a total loss of psychological independence. Grooming is, looked at from one angle, just a particularly intense, blind and irrational form of love. Many women who have been in an abusive relationship will describe the feeling of being hopelessly trapped in the emotional forcefield of their abuser. They are terrified, wretchedly unhappy, but also desperate to stay.

This is very common in the porn industry. On many occasions, women who have worked in porn will, when they're still a part of the industry, tell fans and journalists that they love their work. They will typically only share the dark side of their experiences once they've left. And by then their images are out in the world, and there's no way of getting them back.

Many ex-porn stars now speak candidly about the cruelty of the industry. They say it's racist and financially exploitative. Many of the women catch sexually transmitted diseases. There is a total lack of respect for the boundaries and wellbeing of porn performers. Many of them come away from scenes with injuries and became dependent on drugs and alcohol to numb the physical and emotional pain.

This tendency of porn stars to change their view applies even to the most famous among them. Jenna Jameson, for instance, is still one of the most famous porn actresses in the world. For a time she was one of the porn industry's most visible supporters. She argued in public debates against the idea that porn is harmful.[1]

But Jameson is now a vehement critic of the sex industry. In her autobiography *How to Make Love Like a Porn Star: A Cautionary Tale* she writes of the dark side. She had to have sex with men she found repulsive. She was in near constant physical pain and exhaustion resulting from a gruelling schedule. The industry was filled with abusive men who take any opportunity to degrade the women they work with. Jameson left the sex industry in 2008 and has since become an outspoken conservative and anti-porn campaigner.[2]

The crimes of MindGeek

Jameson's fury is directed in particular at Pornhub, the tenth most visited website in the world. She has lent her support to the American campaign group Traffickinghub, who have been gathering evidence that Pornhub knowingly hosts videos of children and sex trafficking victims being raped.

Globally, the porn industry is certainly worth many billions of US dollars, with some placing the figure as high as $97 billion. MindGeek, the giant of the porn world, operates nearly a hundred websites, including Pornhub, that in total consume more bandwidth than Twitter (now formally known as 'X'), Amazon or Facebook.[3]

MindGeek is a complex organisation that is far from transparent. Its senior executives are not household names.

Consent is not enough

As a result, despite having made a lot of money, they have been able to keep out of the media spotlight (so far). In December 2020, an article in *The New York Times* delivered a painful blow to MindGeek. Nicholas Kristof, a journalist, investigated the failure of Pornhub to remove sexual images of children and non-consenting adults.

The response was immediate. Mastercard and Visa both announced that they would be ending the use of their cards on Pornhub. Four days after the publication of Kristof's piece, MindGeek announced that it would remove 'potentially illegal material', ban downloads, and change its upload policies so that only verified users would be permitted to post videos.[4] Pornhub later purged all existing videos from unverified users, reducing the number of videos on its platform from thirteen million to four million.[5] This was by far the most significant crackdown in the site's history.

It was also not enough. An ongoing legal case gives a taste of MindGeek's shady practices, which may be still be happening, despite the introduction of its new safeguarding measures.

GirlsDoPorn was a porn production company, founded in 2009, whose channel was at one point one of the twenty most popular on Pornhub. These were not amateur videos posted by unverified users. GirlsDoPorn was a slick, professional company that relied on an elaborate scam. They placed fake modelling adverts online asking for young women aged eighteen to twenty-two to contact them. Those who responded were put in touch with other women paid to pretend they had had positive experiences working

Consent is not enough

for the company as models. Some of the women were told part of the truth: that they would be obliged to have sex on camera. But none were told that the videos would be distributed online.

GirlsDoPorn producers lied to these women, telling them that the videos would be sold on DVD to private buyers on the other side of the world. The women were coerced into producing porn that was then distributed without their knowledge. Half of them were not even paid what they been promised.

Some of the GirlsDoPorn producers have now been charged with offences including sex trafficking and producing sexual images of children. A group of forty victims filed a lawsuit in December 2020 claiming that MindGeek knew about the company's sex trafficking from an early stage but nevertheless continued to partner with GirlsDoPorn.[6] The lawsuit also alleges that MindGeek failed to remove GirlsDoPorn videos despite requests for removal by victims. At the time of writing, the lawsuit is still going on.[7]

Despite this kind of barely concealed malpractice, MindGeek continues to churn out profits for one simple reason: people keep watching.

Limbic capitalism

In a 2020 survey of men across a range of Western European countries, respondents reported watching an average of seventy minutes of online porn a week. Two per cent watched more than seven hours.[8] The average man, it seems, spends more time watching porn than he does showering.[9]

And yet, not all men watch porn, including young men. A 2019 BBC survey found that 23 per cent of UK men aged eighteen to twenty-five reported having *not* watched porn in the last month.[10] A minority of people account for the vast majority of porn consumption. It is these consumers who are chiefly responsible for allowing the porn industry to flourish. Yet they are also exploited by the industry in their own way. A lot of porn consumers feel conflicted about their use. A common emotional response among users is a feeling of overwhelming arousal, followed abruptly by feelings of shame immediately after orgasm.

This response is explained by the fact that sexual arousal suppresses our disgust response[11] for a straightforward biological reason. Other people are potential sources of disease, but we have to get close to other people in order to reproduce. The disgust response is therefore disabled when we find those strangers sexually attractive. And the disgust response is very closely linked with moral intuition.[12] Put simply, we're not as good at making subtle moral judgements when we're horny.

And porn sites are set up to arouse users as quickly as possible. The thumbnails show the most explicit moments of a video. The links to videos are also often animated, and play automatically when the user hovers a cursor over them. As soon as a user loads up the website, they are immediately bombarded with intense sexual images. This basic drive, as fundamental as hunger or thirst, can't be resisted through

Consent is not enough

moral reasoning. It is an involuntary response that the porn industry has become very adept at provoking.

This kind of website design is a particularly disturbing example of what David Courtwright, an academic who specialises in the history of drugs, has called 'limbic capitalism'. This means a system whereby businesses make money by encouraging 'excessive consumption and addiction'.[13] They do this 'targeting the limbic system, the part of the brain responsible for feeling'.

Limbic capitalism is why the most successful apps are brightly coloured like fresh fruit and glint like fresh water. Our primitive brains helplessly seek out the stimuli that we have evolved to be attracted to because responding to those stimuli gave our ancestors a survival advantage. Businesses are aware of these instincts and try to exploit them.

Porn is to sex as McDonald's is to food. Both take our natural appetites, pluck out the most compulsive and addictive elements, strip away anything truly nutritious, and then encourage us to consume more and more. Both products are examples of superstimuli: exaggerated versions of naturally occurring stimuli. These tap into an evolved desire for nourishment, excitement and pleasure, but do so in a dangerous way. They fool the consumer into gorging on a product that initially feels good but in the long term does them harm.

When faced with such temptations, we human beings are like the Australian jewel beetle. This is a glossy, golden-coloured beetle around 4cm long. In 1981, insect specialists observed a male jewel beetle attempting to mate with

Consent is not enough

a discarded beer bottle (known in Australian slang as a 'stubbie'). Upon further investigation, they found that male jewel beetles were not only frequently mistaking stubbies for females of their species, they *actually preferred* the stubbies. They ignored actual female beetles in order to hump the glass bottles because these bits of litter were *more* glossy and *more* golden than the female jewel beetles, and thus more sexually exciting to the males.[14]

Porn is similar, which is why some men are already prioritising watching porn over pursuing relationships with real partners. This helps create a situation where the average young person is now having sex less often than their parents and grandparents once did. There is also an increasingly large and frustrated population of men who remain virgins into their twenties and beyond. This subset of men is particularly vulnerable to limbic capitalism. The two per cent of Western European men who report watching more than seven hours of porn a week are not a healthy and happy group. Nor are the men who watch less porn, but are still harmed by it.

The rise of the NoFap movement illustrates the sexual dissatisfaction that porn use causes. Founded in 2011 by the American web developer Alexander Rhodes, NoFap encourages followers to give up both porn and masturbation ('fap' being slang derived from the sound of a man pleasuring himself). It offers its overwhelmingly male followers freedom from the addictive power of porn. It also helps to tackle the fact that porn use has caused rates of sexual dysfunction among young men to rapidly increase.

Consent is not enough

Erectile dysfunction now affects between fourteen and thirty-five per cent of young men, in contrast to perhaps two or three per cent at the beginning of this century.[15]

Members of the NoFap subreddit sometimes write of masturbating so often that they give themselves painful abrasions. Many report suffering from 'death-grip syndrome', a term used to describe the loss of sensation that can sometimes result from masturbating too aggressively. Sufferers report finding it difficult or impossible to reach orgasm during sex with another person. This is partly because of physical desensitisation and partly because of the psychological effect of porn use. Even if they are motivated to seek out sex with a real person, psychological death-grip may mean that they cannot become aroused by someone whose body isn't exactly like that of a porn star. These porn users expose themselves to so much sexual stimulation that they literally become impotent.

The American actor and athlete Terry Crews is now an advocate of the NoFap movement. He has spoken publicly about his own struggle with porn addiction:

> Some people say, 'Hey, man . . . you can't really be addicted to pornography.' But I'm gonna tell you something . . . It changes the way you think about people. People become objects. People become body parts; they become things to be used rather than people to be loved.[16]

Crews is handsome, rich and successful. He is also a husband and father of five. Nevertheless, he found himself neglecting his wife and watching porn instead, like an Australian jewel beetle choosing a stubbie over a real, living mate. Such is the power that porn has over some users.

Increased porn use has had a very odd overall impact. On the one hand, the expectation has become that sex will be aggressive and loveless. But, on the other, we have a group of men who are so desensitised by porn that they (sometimes permanently) are unable to have sexual relationships with real people. Put simply, the porn generation are having *less sex*, and the sex they are having *is also worse*. It's less intimate, less satisfying, and less meaningful.

Logging off

We are rapidly entering a world in which tech dominates the most intimate parts of our lives. This tech is designed by corporations whose sole interest is profit.

There are a few people in the porn industry who are unambiguously villainous – the executives of MindGeek, for example. There are also many more whose moral status is harder to define. In particular, porn users, who are both the drivers of the industry and also its victims.

They are not as victimised as the performers, of course, but they are victimised nonetheless. They are caught up in a form of limbic capitalism that takes our most basic instincts and corrupts them in the pursuit of profit. You cannot criticise capitalism without also criticising the porn industry, which represents the most extreme form of exploitation.

Consent is not enough

And yet, most anti-capitalists prefer to look away. In fact, the most committed defences of porn come nowadays from self-described 'sex positive' Leftists. They claim that any criticism of the *industry* must necessarily be a criticism of its *workers* (funnily enough, they do not make the same defence of industries that rely on sweatshop labour). These apologists are helped most effectively by the progressive story of sexual liberation and consent. It's always there to comfort any porn user who feels discomfort at what they're funding.

Taking a woman at her word when she says 'of course I'm consenting' is appealing because it's easy. It doesn't require us to look too closely at the reality of porn. It means we don't have to think about how we are all capable of hurting or even destroying ourselves. You can do terrible and lasting harm to a 'consenting adult' who is begging you for more.

Some feminists place their faith in so-called 'ethical porn'. In theory, this means porn made in such a way as to avoid the darker and more sexist aspects of the industry.

This is wishful thinking, which distracts from how the porn industry really operates. For one thing, porn marketed as 'ethical' makes up such a tiny and unpopular proportion of the market. Focusing on it is like, as feminist writer Sarah Ditum has put it, 'putting a chicken in your back garden and claiming you've fixed factory farming'.[17] For another, whatever 'ethical' label may be stuck on a video, you cannot look at it and know for sure that the people in it were truly happy to be there. You cannot look at a video and know if

Consent is not enough

the people in it are *still happy* that their images are out in the world.

And even if porn were to be made 'ethically', the product itself will always have a damaging effect on the consumer's sexuality. Porn trains the mind to regard sex as a spectator sport, to be enjoyed alone and in front of a screen. It removes love and mutuality from sex. It turns humans – as Terry Crews has put it – 'into body parts'.

This is one of those rare problems that has such a blindingly simple solution: opt out. Regardless of whether the state regulates the porn industry – as I believe it ought to – the individual can stop watching. There is no good reason to use porn. Giving it up costs the consumer nothing. It is easier by far than giving up factory farmed meat or products made by sweatshop labour. Although we all need to eat and clothe ourselves, not a single one of us needs to watch porn ever again. The sexual liberation narrative tells you to keep going; I'm telling you that you should stop.

VIOLENCE IS NOT LOVE

The publication of *Fifty Shades of Grey* in 2011 marked the moment when BDSM (Bondage, Domination, and Sadomasochism) entered the mainstream. This was a novel themed around a BDSM relationship, written for a female audience. It still holds the UK record for the bestselling paperback of all time.

Christian Grey, the troubled hero of the novel, is charming and handsome. He is also a billionaire, and the victim of his affections, Anastasia, is wooed just as much by his Airbus EC130 helicopter as she is by the sex dungeon that he calls his 'Red Room'. What Christian Grey really does is just domestic abuse. He becomes obsessed with a much younger, virginal woman. He wins her over by bombarding her with attention. He controls her every move, from what she wears to who she spends time with. He even dictates what she's allowed to eat.

And here's the troubling thing: a lot of women loved it. Not all women. Personally, I (and most of my friends) were unmoved by Christian Grey's charms. For a considerable minority, however, the combination of domestic abuse and flashy wealth proved highly arousing.

Some feminists have explained this historically as the product solely of a society that celebrates female submission and male domination. Although there is some truth to this, it doesn't fully explain the popularity of *Fifty Shades*. The sad truth is that a minority of women find BDSM sexy. Some claim that BDSM expresses their sexual freedom. To my mind, a more likely explanation for this behaviour is that some women may be biologically predisposed to find Christian Grey's abusive behaviour arousing.

The idea of possessiveness

In Chapter 2, we saw that there are important average differences between men and women's sexuality. One difference is that women are more preoccupied with partners' displays of emotional loyalty. This is because a pregnant or nursing woman is vulnerable, and she and her baby are more likely to survive if she has a committed and well-resourced mate. A man may demonstrate his commitment by, for example, lavishing his mate with gifts and attention, or being kind to children.

He can also show his commitment in more unpleasant ways. Christian Grey is nasty, but his obsessive behaviour towards Anastasia does at least seem to demonstrate his

Violence is not love

unwavering commitment to her. *Fifty Shades* adds whips and chains, but many older romance novels are similar: a strong handsome man falls passionately in love with the heroine and will do anything to have her, including violence.

Next time you're in your local library, have a look some vintage romance novels – for example, ones published by Mills and Boon. Invariably the heroes are portrayed as big, muscly, and are either high-status professionals (surgeons, say) or adventurous rogues (e.g. pirates). In short, the female readers of erotic fiction have never been turned on by a man who plays hard to get or hesitates. Long before *Fifty Shades*, what these readers were aroused by is the fantasy of a man who is *really into them,* often obsessively so.

The tragedy is that, while the fictional Christian Grey may be faithful to Anastasia, his real-life counterpart often isn't. It's easy enough for an inexperienced or overly trusting woman to confuse jealousy for fidelity and so be drawn to aggressive heroes. But in reality, jealous men are rarely faithful.

The psychiatrist Theodore Dalrymple has written about his experiences of working at a hospital in a deprived area of Birmingham, England, where he often encountered both the victims and perpetrators of domestic abuse:

The great majority of the jealous men I meet are flagrantly unfaithful to the object of their supposed affections, and some keep other women in the same jealous subjection elsewhere in the city and even a hundred miles away. They have no compunction

Violence is not love

about cuckolding other men and actually delight in doing so as a means of boosting their own fragile egos. As a result, they imagine that all other men are their rivals: for rivalry is a reciprocal relationship. Thus, a mere glance in a pub directed at a man's girlfriend is sufficient to start a fight not only between the girl and her lover but, even before that, between the two men.[1]

As for the women who become involved with such men, Dalrymple writes of a self-harming instinct which is not often acknowledged among feminists. It is, however, likely to be familiar to anyone who has ever worked with victims of domestic abuse:

> But why does the woman not leave the man as soon as he manifests his violence? It is because, perversely, violence is the only token she has of his commitment to her. Just as he wants the exclusive sexual possession of her, she wants a permanent relationship with him. She imagines – falsely – that a punch in the face or a hand round the throat is at least a sign of his contin-ued interest in her, the only sign other than sexual intercourse she is ever likely to receive in that regard.[2]

In this chapter, I'm going to argue that BDSM is simply a new, glamorised version of this sort of this violence. As we will see, BDSM enthusiasts have tried to present their sexual interest as politically radical but, in fact, it is nothing of the sort.

Violence is not love

The mainstreaming of BDSM has, firstly, served to protect the interests of men who want to beat up women and avoid being punished for it. It has also made a lot of money for the porn industry and for manufacturers of tacky leather clothing. In other words, BDSM is good for abusive men, and good for business. It is not radical.

The popular representation of BDSM often focuses on a very unusual relationship in which a wealthy businessman pays a female dominatrix for regular whippings. These relationships do exist, but they are not typical.

Most submissives ('subs') are female and most dominants ('doms') are male. One study[3] found that only 34 per cent of men consistently preferred being the sub, while an even smaller proportion of women – eight per cent – identified as doms. The same study found that doms tended to be low in the agreeableness personality trait (i.e. they were assertive and demanding). Subs, in contrast, tended to be more agreeable than average. They are eager to please. Most of the time, doms remain doms outside of the bedroom (or sex dungeon), and subs remain subs. In the real world, BDSM does not defy the sexual domination of women by men, as some of its defenders claim – rather, *it reinforces it*.

Choking

Unfortunately, most twenty-first-century feminists are under the impression that BDSM represents a kind of sexual liberation for women, if everyone is consenting. Liberal feminists insist that, so long as someone consents

Violence is not love

and their partner will stop when asked, hurting or humiliating a woman is fine.[4]

Of all of the sex acts associated with BDSM, strangulation is currently the most fashionable and also the most gendered. In porn, men strangle men, men strangle women, but women are very rarely the ones doing the strangling. Strangulation *outside of sex* is also gendered, with the vast majority of victims being female and the vast majority of perpetrators being male. One study in San Diego found that, of three hundred forensic records reporting strangulation, 298 involved a man strangling a woman. And it is a crime that is very often suffered by victims of domestic violence, most of whom are women.

The UK domestic abuse charity Refuge reports that 48 per cent of women using their services report having been strangled, choked or suffocated. Women who have previously been strangled by their partners are eight times more likely to be killed by them, often by strangulation, since this is the second most common method of murder used by men against women in the UK.[5] Scroll through 'choking' porn and you'll seeing many images of men with their hands around women's throats. Anyone not trained in the ideology of liberal feminism would be forgiven for seeing nothing more than bog-standard male violence against women. This is the kind of violence that feminists are supposed to be united against.

The trend for sexual strangulation is not confined to porn. Research has found that over half of 18-to-24-year-old UK women reported having been strangled by their part-

Violence is not love

ners during sex. This compares to 23 per cent of women in the oldest age group surveyed, aged 35 to 39.[6] Many of these respondents reported that this experience had been unwanted and frightening, but others reported that they had consented to it, or even invited it.

And here lies the complication, because you don't have to look hard to find women who say they love being strangled. The argument from liberal feminists is that, since there are some women who enjoy being strangled, it is wrong to condemn all strangulation: only non-consensual strangulation is wrong.

In July 2020, for instance, *Men's Health* magazine ran a feature titled 'Breath Play Is a Popular Form of BDSM. Here's How to Do It Safely.'[7] When Member of Parliament Laura Farris criticised the article for being anti-feminist, she was met with a huge backlash on Twitter (X), largely from young women who insisted that consensual strangulation is a harmless form of kink.

But they are wrong. An alarming study from 2020 reveals the injuries that can be caused by non-fatal strangulation, including cardiac arrest, stroke, miscarriage, speech disorders, seizures, paralysis, and other forms of long-term brain injury.[8] Although it takes several minutes actually to kill someone by strangulation, unconsciousness can occur within seconds, and always indicates at least a mild brain injury. The injuries caused by strangulation may not be immediately visible to the naked eye. They are therefore far less obvious than injuries like broken bones, and so may be missed during a police investigation.

Violence is not love

The idea that strangulation can ever be done safely is an urban myth. Scientist Helen Bichard has said, 'I cannot see a way of safely holding a neck so that you wouldn't be pressing on any fragile structures.'[9] And, given that the possible consequences of strangulation are not widely understood, Bichard argues that most people are not capable of giving truly informed consent to it.

Sadly, messages and images shared or liked by women on social media and testimony that I've heard directly from young women suggest that many of the women who seek out strangulation have a very misguided understanding of what strangulation *means* when men do it to them during sex.

To put it bluntly, many of these women are deluded. They think strangulation indicates a man's love and desire for them. It usually indicates none of these things, but in a society in which the myth *of Fifty Shades of Grey* is popular, it shouldn't surprise us that many misinterpret aggression from their male partners as a sign of passion. The truth is that real-life Christian Greys usually have no interest whatsoever in the wellbeing of the women they abuse.

We can't consent to this

Even if you accept the liberal feminist claim that it is possible for someone to truly consent to being strangled by their sexual partner, you are still faced with a problem. How is the law supposed to differentiate between consensual and non-consensual instances of sexual violence? A consensual

Violence is not love

BDSM relationship and an abusive relationship look can have exactly the same physical effects. So if a sub is injured or killed during sex, and her dom claims it was an accident, how exactly are the courts supposed to tell the difference?

This is not a theoretical problem. The *We Can't Consent To This* campaign, which I've worked on, has documented sixty-seven cases in the UK in which people have been killed and their killers have claimed that their deaths were the result of a sex game 'gone wrong'. All suspects in these killings have so far been male and sixty of those killed have been female. Most of the victims died from strangulation, and most of the victims were the wives or girlfriends of perpetrators. Often there was evidence of domestic abuse. Other women had only met the perpetrators that day and many victims were involved in the sex trade.

There are two striking trends in the data we've collected. Firstly, the number of rough sex cases has increased significantly since the turn of this century. Secondly, defendants who rely on this defence have increasingly got off: roughly half of these homicide cases have resulted in murder conviction. Within the last two decades, courts have become much more willing to believe defendants when they claim that their victims died because they literally 'asked for it'.

Feminists in other parts of the world have also documented a rise in the use of the rough sex defence, with similar cases found in Canada,[10] Italy,[11] Russia,[12] Mexico,[13] Germany[14] and the United States.[15] The increasing success of the 'rough sex defence' internationally seems to be

Violence is not love

a result of the fact that courts are increasingly willing to believe that women not only consent to, but *actually seek out*, the kind of violence that can prove lethal. This is one consequence of the normalisation of BDSM.

This normalisation is glaringly obvious online, where BDSM content, often strangulation-themed, has migrated from niche porn sites, to mainstream porn sites, and now to social media. This includes platforms that advertise themselves as suitable for children aged thirteen and over. On these platforms, strangulation of women is presented as loving, sexy, desirable, and sometimes amusing. The images are almost always taken from the perspective of the person doing the strangling.

You do not have to go searching for these images. If you are exposed to mainstream porn or even just to mainstream social media, you are very likely to come across them accidentally. A recent newspaper article quotes a young student who reports that she started seeing strangulation material on Tumblr from the age of fourteen:

> I'd inadvertently see a lot of pornographic material because accounts would use the hashtags of other popular TV shows or media to bring followers to their porn sites . . . After my experiences with Tumblr, I felt that choking was normalised as a sexual behaviour. It's shown as an expression of passion and it's something that girls are kind of groomed into doing, but it's only recently that I see that being critiqued as something criminal.[16]

Violence is not love

Porn platforms profit from a process of escalation, introducing users to milder content, and then – for those who are susceptible – suggesting more and more extreme and addictive content as the viewer is gradually desensitised. For many users, this leads inexorably towards BDSM.

Is it really plausible that all of these young people spontaneously decided that strangulation was fun and sexy? Or could the fact that this generation is the first to have been raised on online porn be playing a role? This is hard to prove for certain either way. There is no absolutely certain way to prove the link between porn use and sexual behaviour, says Clare McGlynn, Professor of Law at Durham University. But McGlynn draws a comparison with advertising:

> It's not that I watch adverts and then go out and buy a particular washing powder. But on some level it is having some influence on me, and companies spend billions on advertising.[17]

The comparison is a good one, but it also returns us to the troubling issue that I raised in the last chapter. Companies selling washing powder *are responding to demand*, and so are porn producers.

Strangulation is a fashion spread by porn, but it is based on something that the porn industry did not create: violent men who are aroused by domination, and insecure women who seek it out. It is the same theme we see in *Fifty Shades*, and sometimes in older novels. It isn't new, but it has been horribly exaggerated in the modern world.

Violence is not love

And the liberal feminist appeal to consent isn't good enough. It cannot account for the ways in which the sexuality of impressionable young people can be warped by porn or other forms of cultural influence. It cannot convincingly explain why a woman who hurts *herself* should be understood as mentally ill, but a woman who asks *her partner* to hurt her is apparently not. Above all, the liberal feminist faith in consent relies on a fundamentally false idea: that who we are in the bedroom is different from who we are outside of it.

In a recent piece, the *Sunday Times'* advice columnist Dolly Alderton repeated this foolish idea in her response to a letter by a 29-year-old woman concerned that she was repeatedly 'drawn to' misogynist men:

> I think everyone should be free to separate their sexuality from their politics, as long as every party has consented and is having fun. What's important is that you don't confuse your craving for sexual objectification or domination with a need for a misogynistic or dominating boyfriend . . . Put simply: you need a kind, chill, respectful boyfriend in the streets and a filthy pervert in the sheets. They do exist. I hope you have fun finding one.[18]

Alderton's recommendation was that her respondent seek out casual sex on dating apps with men who are willing to act like dominating misogynists in the bedroom, but who are also 'nice'. It's terrible advice. Liberal feminists like

Violence is not love

Alderton are effectively telling young women to meet up for sex, via the internet, with strange men who like violence.

Any man who can maintain an erection while beating up his partner is a man to steer well clear of. But BDSM enthusiasts don't want to hear this grim truth. So the palatable option for liberal feminism is to draw a bright line between a person's sexuality and their personality. The problem is that while masochistic women may want to *play at* being raped, they do not want to *actually be raped*. And yet seeking out a man who is turned on by violence may well result in exactly this. If you go looking for a man who is turned on by rape, he is likely to rape you.

The liberal feminist analysis of sexual violence is not only wrong, but dangerous. It tells people – mostly men – that if they discover in themselves a desire to hurt other people, they shouldn't resist it, but should instead cultivate it. And it tells others – mostly women – with masochistic impulses that these desires, too, should be encouraged. That instead of running in terror from violent men, they should stay and give the sadist exactly what he wants, until one day his desires are no longer confined to the bedroom, and he no longer stops at 'no'.

PEOPLE ARE NOT PRODUCTS

As we have seen, evolved differences between men and women have created a 'sexuality gap'. This means that, on average, men are much more likely than women to desire casual sex. This creates a mismatch, because there are a lot more straight men looking for casual sex than straight women. This means that many of these men are left frustrated by the lack of willing casual partners.

In the post-sexual revolution era, the solution to this mismatch has often been to encourage women (ideally young, attractive ones) to overcome their reluctance and to have casual sex on a large scale, like men. My argument is that this has been falsely presented as a form of sexual liberation for women, when in fact it is nothing of the sort. It serves male interests, not female. However, although this is true, it does not mean that how things were done in the past was ideal. All societies must find some kind of solution

People are not products

to the sexuality gap, and those solutions can be anti-woman in many ways.

Our modern solution is to encourage *all* women, from every class, to meet the male demand for casual sex. In contrast, the solution adopted by most societies before reliable contraception was invented was different. The *majority* of women had sex only within marriage, while *a minority* of poor women (prostitutes) were forced to meet the 'excess' male demand for casual sex.

Although there have been a tiny number of high-status prostitutes in history, most have been women with no other options, like the very poor, drug and alcohol addicts, and slaves. Prostitution is the ancient solution to the sexuality gap, and it is not a pleasant one.

Many modern liberal feminists have claimed that selling sex is fine. They say it's no different from selling any other product. If this is the case, why would the vast majority of women only ever become prostitutes if they were so poor and desperate that they had no other option, except death? Liberal feminists say that the reason is that prostitution is stigmatised. This, they argue, makes life difficult and dangerous for prostitutes. Both of these claims are true. So why did the stigma arise in the first place? They often claim that the stigma arose purely because Western societies were negative and puritanical about sex, and, due to the patriarchy, particularly about women's sexuality.[1]

This is a very odd claim. The 'patriarchy' (a social system that prioritises male interests over female) does not necessarily demand the stigmatisation of female sexuality at all,

People are not products

at least not consistently. Men might not want *their* wives or daughters to have illicit sex, but they are often quite happy for the wives and daughters of *other* men to do so. This means that reserving a prostituted class for the purposes of male enjoyment suits male interests very nicely. Why, then, would patriarchy explain the intense and universal reluctance that women almost always feel when faced with the prospect of becoming a prostitute?

There is a much more convincing explanation for the deep disgust that women typically feel about becoming prostitutes. As we saw earlier, women are the ones who bear the very heavy physical cost of reproduction: they get pregnant, grow the baby inside them, give birth, and nurse the child. Given this, is it any surprise that women are picky about who they have sex with? Before contraception (99%+ of human history), the decision to have sex was far more consequential for a woman than it was for a man. The possibility of an unwanted pregnancy left her with very difficult options. She had to raise the baby without support from a mate, attempt abortion, try and find an adoptive family, or kill the baby. No woman can just up and leave, like men can.

The Pill has existed for seventy years, while *Homo sapiens* has existed for approximately 200,000 years. We evolved in an environment in which sex led to pregnancy, and the ways we evolved to respond to this remain with us. Of course, nature *can* be overcome, to an extent. We all live modern lives that are very different from those of our ancient ancestors. It is, however, very hard to remove deeply embedded adaptations from the human mind.

People are not products

Emotionally, if not legally, it is difficult to distinguish prostitution from rape. The feminist campaigner Rachel Moran, who was in prostitution from the age of fifteen through to twenty-two, describes her own emotional response as identical to that experienced during sexual abuse:

> I felt the same sickening nausea and rising panic that is inherent to conventional sexual abuse in each prostitution experience I ever had, and I felt that regardless of whether or not a man stayed within the agreed sexual boundaries . . . When we understand that the sex paid for in prostitution shares so many of its characteristics with the sex stolen in rape, it makes sense that so many prostituted women make clear parallels between the two experiences.[2]

The whole point of paid sex is that it must be paid. It is not mutually desired by both parties. One party is there unwillingly, in exchange for (usually) money. The person being paid must ignore her own lack of sexual desire, or even her bone-deep revulsion. She must suppress her self-protective instincts in the service of another person's sexual pleasure. This is why the sex industry typically attracts only the poorest and the most desperate women. They have no other choice.

$20 and $200

Politics becomes odd when we debate the sex industry. Usually, people who identify with the Left are concerned

People are not products

with championing the interests of the poor and exploited. But, when it comes to prostitution, that position is reversed. Rather than talking about the women at the bottom of the industry – the very poor, drug addicted, or trafficked – liberal feminists do the opposite. They talk about and ally themselves with those at the top of the industry.

I don't dispute that there are some self-described sex workers who are not in poverty. Some support the decriminalisation of prostitution and insist that sex work is just like any other kind of work. These women are particularly prominent in the media and on platforms like Twitter (X). They are not like the vast majority of prostitutes. They tend to be white, Western, and university educated. They are not the ones whose lives are tightly controlled by their pimp, or who can't speak English. They are representative only of the most comparatively lucky end of the sex industry.

In contrast, the women who campaign for the so-called Nordic Model, which criminalises buyers and pimps but decriminalises sellers, tend to be very different. They are much more likely to have left the sex industry before speaking out, and to have been in brothel and street-based prostitution, rather than escorting or working on sex cams. They are also much more likely to have been born in poverty.

The point here is not that educated or middle-class people's views are irrelevant because of their class background. I myself am educated and middle class. The point is that your economic position has a profound effect on your personal preferences. Once you start paying attention, you notice how many pro-sex-work activists have had an unu-

People are not products

sual experience of the sex industry. Julie Bindel, the investigative journalist and campaigner against sexual violence, writes of some of the most prominent voices in media discussions of the sex industry:

> Many of those high-profile pro-prostitution lobbyists who speak as 'sex workers' are what I would call 'tourists'. Melissa Gira-Grant for example, who is highly educated and earning her living as a journalist; Brooke Magnanti, who holds a PhD, has written several books, and works as a scientist; and Douglas Fox, whose partner owns one of the largest escort agencies in Britain, are not representative of the sex trade.[3]

It's easy for people who are highly untypical of the sex industry to pose as typical because the term 'sex worker' has such a loose meaning. Sometimes it might refer to – as in Magnanti's case – actually having sex with clients. Others – like Gira-Grant – may have only ever done cam work. Douglas Fox is able to describe himself as an 'independent male sex worker', and can even retain a prominent position in the International Union of Sex Workers, despite the fact that he is actually a pimp.[4] Academics writing on these topics also often describe themselves as 'sex workers', while being deliberately vague about what they really mean by that.

This is a longstanding issue in the sex workers' rights movement. One of the first and most influential organisations in favour of the full decriminalisation of prostitution

People are not products

was COYOTE (Call Off Your Old Tired Ethics). COYOTE was founded in San Francisco in 1973, and often described in the media as 'the first prostitutes' union'.[5] But, when the sociologist Elizabeth Bernstein studied prostitutes in San Francisco, she found COYOTE members to be highly unrepresentative:

> The vast majority of COYOTE's members are white, middle-class and well-educated, just as their political opponents claim . . . Many work out of expensively furnished homes or rented 'work spaces' by placing advertisements in newspapers, earning enough money not only to cover expenses, but also to help finance alternative artistic and intellectual careers . . . The average hourly fee, whether or not one is 'in business for herself', is $200.

This is in contrast to the prostitutes Bernstein described as being at 'the other end of the continuum': homeless women, addicted to crack or heroin, who would sell sex for $20 and then immediately spend the proceeds on drugs. Most of these women were tightly controlled by pimps and were visibly sickly and distressed.[6]

This account draws attention to a problem that typically goes unacknowledged in debates on the sex industry. Those who support decriminalising sex work say 'listen to sex workers'. But *which ones?*

106

People are not products

Luxury beliefs

The psychologist Rob Henderson has invented the term 'luxury beliefs'.[7] He argues that rich people are now less likely to associate being high status with owning certain things, but rather having certain far-fetched opinions. These opinions tend to be things that, if enacted, would harm the poor, but sound very radical. Examples would be supporting the abolition of the police or the legalisation of hard drugs. Having crime run riot in poor areas or drug addiction going up would be highly likely to harm poor people, but would not affect the rich. So, such opinions are used by the rich to signal their superiority over the poor.

Among those in high-status, educated professions (like the media or universities), repeating a phrase like 'sex work is work' gives the speaker high status. It suggests an admirable open mindedness and a rebellious attitude towards traditional sexual morals. These ideas are highly prized in these circles.

Proponents of this luxury belief may share hashtags like #supportsexworkers on Twitter (X). They will tell anyone who disagrees with them to 'listen to sex workers', but they will typically never have met or spoken with anyone who has experienced prostitution. But, since the term 'sex worker' is vague and general, the difference between poor and relatively privileged prostitutes is obscured.

However, that doesn't mean that the class distinctions go away. Support for the decriminalisation of prostitution may

People are not products

not obviously *look* like a luxury belief. Its supporters will typically use terms like 'oppression' and 'marginalisation'. But in effect *it is* a luxury belief, since the costs are not borne by the upper classes who gain status by supporting the idea. They are borne by the lower-class people – overwhelmingly women – who are most likely actually to end up in the sex industry.

Decriminalisation of the sex industry leads to more people paying for sex. In countries that have done it, the proportion of men who have ever bought sex is higher, and the sex tourism industry is larger. Given that the number of women who will willingly enter the sex trade is very small, when demand grows, unwilling women must be sought out in order to meet it.

Selling sex is risky. Prostitutes are far more likely to be murdered,[8] or die from drug or alcohol abuse than other women.[9] But some defend prostitution by arguing that it is not the only sort of work that is dangerous. Brook Magnanti, for instance, a former escort, compares a career selling sex to a career as a deep-sea fishermen. She argues that they are both dangerous but legitimate forms of work.[10]

This sort of argument leads us to talk as if prostitution is like any other business. Pimps and madams engage in 'sex-work management',[11] rape becomes a 'contract breach',[12] and violence, pregnancy and disease become 'occupational health risks'.[13] The horror of what is actually happening is deliberately obscured. Those who support sex work want us to resist our emotional impulses. They want us to see

People are not products

prostitution as much the same as deep-sea fishing, only with an added layer of pointless stigma – a relic from less enlightened times.

The redistribution of sex

Sexual disenchantment is a term I have borrowed from Aaron Sibarium. It means the idea that sex 'has no inherent value beyond what consenting adults assign to it'. This means that 'a marriage, a one-night stand, a "throuple", a hook-up, [or] a brothel . . . are all equally valid means of getting sex'.[14]

Liberal feminists hold sexual disenchantment as an article of faith. They insist that it is *a good thing* that sex is now regarded as without inherent value. But, in practice, liberal feminist women do not generally behave as if they believe this. Almost no one does.

Sexual disenchantment is often appealed to by those who support the decriminalisation of prostitution. It is common to hear them compare sex work to other forms of work and challenge their critics to name the difference. They assume that this move will work because all 'good liberals' believe in sexual disenchantment.

But even the best liberals do still *feel* that sex is somehow different, even if they struggle to say why. People care if their partner has sex with someone else, and not only because doing so involves breaking a promise. People know intuitively that a boss asking for sex in exchange for a promotion is entirely different from a boss asking for overtime in exchange for a promotion.

People are not products

Indeed, it is odd that so many liberal feminists who argue that 'sex work is work' are hyper-sensitive to any hint of sexual impropriety in their own workplaces. These women recoil at being asked out for dinner by a male colleague, or being touched casually on an arm or leg. They describe such acts as 'sexual harassment'. But if *that* is sexual harassment, then how should we describe what goes on in a brothel?

Cynically, I suspect that the different attitude towards these two kinds of workplaces comes down to self-interest. I don't mean to suggest that middle and upper-class women don't suffer from the costs of the sexual revolution, because of course they do. Hook-up culture also has a pernicious effect on Ivy League and Russell Group campuses, and the boyfriends of economically privileged women are just as likely to be addled by porn as any other men.

But there are certain forms of sexual harm that are far more threatening to people who are simultaneously young, female *and poor*. Prostitution is one of them. And it is telling that when the terrible consequences of sexual disenchantment are likely to personally affect women who are not otherwise at risk of ending up in prostitution, the inconsistency is laid bare.

Take as an example the panic around incels. Incels are involuntarily celibate men who gather online to complain about their lack of success in attracting girlfriends. In 2018, the economist Robin Hanson wrote a blog post about incels. He argued that it is plausible to say that 'that those with much less access to sex suffer to a similar degree as those with low income'.[15] As a result, why shouldn't they politi-

People are not products

cally organise, like poor people do, to attempt to secure the 'redistribution' of sex? Or at least to receive money to compensate for not getting any? All hell broke loose on progressive media. *Slate* asked if Hanson was 'America's Creepiest Economist'[16] and Moira Donegan in *Cosmopolitan* expressed outrage:

> Central to the incel ideology is the idea that sex with another person – specifically, penetrative sex with women – isn't a privilege for men, but a right. Incels talk about sex with 'Stacys', their term for attractive women, the way that more reasonable people talk about food, water, and shelter: as a basic necessity for survival . . . Women are not interchangeable, we are not commodities.[17]

Obviously I agree. I don't think that incels are owed sexual access to anyone, whether or not 'cash is redistributed in compensation'.

But note the difference in tone between a passage like this – '*we* don't owe you sex' and '*our* vaginas' – compared to other progressive pieces on sex work, including those written by Donegan. When it's poor prostitutes whose bodies are seen as 'commodities', progressives accept this. They just want to regulate the sex industry to reduce harm. When it's potentially their bodies that might become a commodity, suddenly sexual disenchantment is forgotten, to be replaced by pure rage. *How dare* incels think that beautiful women would even give them the time of day?

People are not products

This is the rage that comes from knowing, deep down, that sex *is* different from other forms of social interaction. Selling sex is inherently different from any other kind of act. Vednita Carter, prostitution survivor and anti-sex trafficking activist, puts the point succinctly: 'people ask me "what is the inherent harm of prostitution?" – the inherent harm is the sex act itself'.[18]

Cultural death grip syndrome

We already talked about 'Death grip syndrome', where men find it difficult to have sex with real people because the intense sexual images from porn have desensitised them. So porn causes people to have *less* sex with real people, while simultaneously exposing them to *more* intense sexual stimuli.

This applies more broadly. Public life has become ever more hyper-sexualised. As a result, we are now routinely exposed to so many sexual images in the course of daily life that they no longer have much effect on us.

In 1994, the company Wonderbra released a now-famous advert (the 'Hello Boys' ad). It depicted beautiful model Eva Herzigová admiring her own boosted cleavage. Posters of this were so distracting to motorists that they reportedly caused car crashes. In contrast, try walking down any British high street today and keep a tally of how many lingerie-clad boobs and bums you see within ten minutes. You see them in shop windows, on the sides of buses, and on the covers of magazines. In a free market, with no moral restraints, sexualisation will go in one direction, and one direction

People are not products

only, and for a simple reason: sex sells, and businesses know it.

Occasionally, a new cultural event will be sufficiently extreme to attract attention. A recent example is the music video for the song WAP ('Wet Ass Pussy'), by the American rappers Cardi B and Megan Three Stallion. Liberal commentators praised this explicit and porn-influenced video as 'an unabashed celebration of female sexuality'.[19]

But this was a strange kind of celebration. The song sees sex as a cash transaction. The male object of lust described in the lyrics is assessed according to the size of his 'king cobra' and the size of his bank balance. 'Pay my tuition', pleads Megan to this imagined man. 'Ask for a car' during sex, 'spit on his mic' to secure a record deal, and so on – the sexual generosity described is all in service, not of female pleasure, but material gain.

WAP has very little to do with real female sexuality, but it does provide a revealing insight into the worst side of *male* sexuality. Although almost no women really believe in the idea of sexual disenchantment, there is a minority of men who do believe in it, at least up to a point. They care about youth, and they care about looks. Apart from that, they don't care who they're ejaculating into, and they certainly don't care if that person is enjoying themselves.

This is a form of male sexuality that many women do not understand, since it is so different from typical female sexuality. But anyone who questions its existence should

People are not products

take a look at the comments that men leave on sites like Punternet, which are dedicated to customer reviews of prostitutes.[20] They don't make for nice reading.

A culture so soaked with porn puts the logic of these men in charge. It takes a – frankly – psychopathic view of human sexuality and allows it to infect everything. It treats people as replaceable and interchangeable. They become merely a collection of relevant body parts. A tongue that could belong to anyone licking the inside of a mouth that could belong to anyone. It is sex stripped down to its barest mechanics.

'Thanks to OnlyFans'

Only a culture dominated by the worst of male sexuality could have eroticised the dick pic and its amputated female counterparts. I don't know what men think we are supposed to do with their dick pics, but I know of no woman who would masturbate to an image in which the rest of the person has been cropped away.

But the internet abounds with them. Many young women on social media now post 'belfies' (butt selfies). Instagram and TikTok, in particular, are filled with the youthful breasts and buttocks of women desperate for some positive male attention.

For some of these women, posting such images leads them towards setting up an account on OnlyFans. This is a platform that allows 'creators' (overwhelmingly women) to earn money by giving 'users' (overwhelmingly men)

114

People are not products

subscription access to online content. Most of it is pornographic. If you are already used to marketing sexy photos of yourself for 'likes', marketing those photos for money may not seem like such a big step. And the incentives seem attractive. Every now and again, a tweet by a previously unknown OnlyFans creator will go viral, as she shares photos of the house she has been able to buy 'thanks to OnlyFans'.

But such rags-to-riches cases are very unusual.[21] The distribution of income on OnlyFans is highly unequal. The most popular one per cent of creators make 33 per cent of all the money. The tiny minority of creators who do well on the site are mostly existing celebrities. The women who post 'thanks to OnlyFans' success stories on social media are not at all representative of ordinary creators. They are rather more like very lucky gamblers.

In fact, most of the women on OnlyFans probably make a loss, given the amount of time they must spend creating content and engaging with users. The average creator attracts only thirty subscribers, but she carries just as much risk of public exposure and harassment as the most successful ones. OnlyFans is not anything like as dangerous as most prostitution – it's definitely more like $200 prostitution than $20 – but it does come with perils, primarily to a woman's long-term relationship prospects, and therefore her long-term happiness.

As I laid out in Chapter 4, most men take a very negative attitude towards what they consider to be a history of promiscuity in a potential marriage partner. So, although an

People are not products

OnlyFans account may provide a woman with short-term self-esteem, and perhaps also cash, it will also limit the pool of men who are willing to marry her. And there are other costs associated with turning yourself into a sexual commodity.

Tinder and its rivals are similar to shopping sites. Their format encourages users to browse the available products and select what they prefer from the comfort of their homes, with little effort, and no intimacy whatsoever.

In a 2015 article on dating apps in *Vanity Fair*, one male user describes the attitude that the apps encourage:

> Guys view everything as a competition. 'Who's slept with the best, hottest girls?' With these dating apps, he says, 'you're always sort of prowling. You could talk to two or three girls at a bar and pick the best one, or you can swipe a couple hundred people a day – the sample size is so much larger. It's setting up two or three Tinder dates a week and, chances are, sleeping with all of them, so you could rack up 100 girls you've slept with in a year.'

Another man directly compared Tinder to an online food delivery service, 'but you're ordering a person'.[22] This is, in his view, a good thing.

And yet, despite all this convenience, Tinder causes its users more unhappiness than almost any other app.[23] Users report that dating apps manage to turn what should be

People are not products

an exciting experience into a dull one, because too many options does not increase the sexual thrill, but instead kills it. Street and brothel-based prostitution is dangerous and traumatic. Let me stress that. But I think I need to warn against the consequences of sexual disenchantment that go beyond the obvious.

On a personal level, we can't just refuse to participate in the sex industry and then pat ourselves on the back for a job well done. Refusing to view people as products goes further than just not buying sex or refusing to use porn. It demands that we challenge the disenchanted idea of what sex ought to be.

The many articles with headlines like '8 Very Necessary Sex Tips From Sex Workers'[24] betray a view of sex that has becoming disturbingly common. Sex workers can act as sources of sex advice only if we understand sex to be a skill that must be learned as a matter of technique. Sex becomes something that one does *to* another person, not *with* another person. All of the emotion is drained away. It becomes cold and clinical.

We must resist this at all costs. If we try and pretend that sex has no special value that makes it different from other acts, then we end up in some very dark places. If sex isn't worthy of its own moral category, then nor is sexual harassment or rape. If we accept that sex is merely a service that can be freely bought and sold, then we have no arguments left to make against the incels who want to 'redistribute' it. If we voice no objection to the principle of 'sex sells', then we can hardly complain when we find ourselves scrolling

People are not products

through would-be sexual partners on a dating app in the same way that we scroll through fast food options. Once you permit the idea that people can be products, everything is corroded.

MARRIAGE IS GOOD

In making the case against the sexual revolution, I've often run across a particular kind of problem. I call it the problem of normal distribution. The normal distribution is also known as the bell curve because the graph it produces looks rather like a bell.

It's best illustrated by taking an example. If you plot a random selection of, say, adult men's heights, and then look at where most of them cluster, you'll find it's around the middle. The majority of men – about two-thirds – are between 5 feet 7 and 6 feet tall. Hardly any man is 6 feet 9 or 4 feet 10. The further a height is away from the average, the less likely it is to occur. This is 'normal distribution'. It's very common in science.[1]

Social phenomena are a little more complicated, but it often applies there too. Sociosexuality (an interest in sexual variety), for instance, is close to being normally distributed.

Marriage is good

Most people are close to average, and a minority of unusual people are found at one or other pole. This means that there are some people who have no interest whatsoever in casual sex, and some people who are off-the-charts horny.

Importantly, though – as I first laid out in Chapter 2 – the bell curves for men and for women are different, with the male average further towards the higher end of the socio-sexuality spectrum. This means that there are a lot more super-horny men than there are women, and a lot more super-not-horny women than there are men.

The problem of normal distribution is this: when you impose some change on a population, different people will experience it differently. It is very, very difficult to design a policy that will home in on just one group of people at just one point on the graph, leaving the rest of the curve unchanged. And, when it comes to a big historical event like the sexual revolution – which nobody designed, or even fully foresaw – that difficulty is increased.

Marital satisfaction is (almost) normally distributed.[2] Most people report being quite happy in their marriages, with a minority who report being very happy, and another minority who report being very unhappy. It used to be exceptionally difficult for those very unhappy couples to divorce. So, if you sought a divorce during this period, it was almost certainly because you were at the very unhappy tail of the normal distribution. You were therefore definitely deserving of help and sympathy.

That was certainly the attitude of the social reformers who began to campaign for loosening divorce laws in

Marriage is good

the years following the Second World War. From roughly the 1960s onwards it suddenly became much easier to get divorced in the West. People who had been legally trapped in hellish marriages were freed from them, which was a good thing. But then came the problem of normal distribution.

The key law that made it easier to get divorced in the UK was the 1969 Divorce Reform Act. If you read the debates in parliament about it, it does not appear that the supporters of the Bill knew what was coming.[3] They believed that their reforms would be an act of kindness towards the small number of people in very unhappy marriages, but that others would be unaffected.

This is not what happened. In the decade following the Divorce Reform Act, the number of divorces trebled and then kept rising, peaking in the 1980s.[4] Since then, there has been a slight decline in the divorce rate. This is not because marriages are now likely to last longer. It's because you can't get divorced if you don't get married in the first place, and marriage rates are at an historic low.[5] In 1968, eight per cent of children were born to parents who were not married; in 2019, it was almost fifty per cent.[6] Today, there are just two marriages for every divorce in the UK each year.[7] Marriage, as it once was, is now more-or-less dead.

In the United States it is deader still. There, almost half of marriages end in divorce.[8] There is also a new and big class divide. Before the 1970s, the vast majority of Americans got married and stayed married, regardless of family income. Now, of those Americans in the top third income bracket,

Marriage is good

64 per cent are in an intact marriage, meaning they have only married once and are still in their first marriage. In contrast, only 24 per cent of Americans in the lower-third income bracket are in an intact marriage.[9] A lasting marriage is fast becoming a luxury for the rich.

Of course, some marriages should end, and in those cases loosening divorce laws was a blessing. Although married women are not at greater risk of domestic violence than unmarried women – the opposite, in fact[10] – it is obviously better when abused wives do not face serious legal obstacles to leave their husbands. The extremely unhappy tail of the normal distribution really did need to get divorced and, before the reforms of the mid-twentieth century, they often couldn't.

But the problem of normal distribution made it impossible for the reforms to laser in on these extreme cases. Most modern divorces are not a consequence of domestic abuse.[11] Most involve a couple growing apart, falling out of love, and trying for a fresh start. But in many of these cases, the promise of happier alternative relationships remains unfulfilled, particularly for women, who are more likely than men to remain permanently single following divorce.[12] What's more, between a third and a half of divorced people in the UK report in surveys that they regret their decision to divorce.[13] There is a lot of space between 'happy' and 'miserably unhappy'. In the past, many in those middling marriages remained married; now they usually don't.

And, in a culture of high divorce rates, even those marriages that last risk being undermined. When marriage

Marriage is good

vows are no longer truly binding, couples seem to become less confident in their relationships. One study found that marital investment declined in the wake of no-fault divorce laws.[14] Newlywed couples in states that passed no-fault divorce were about ten per cent less likely to support a spouse through college or graduate school. They were six per cent less likely to have a child together.

When marriage became impermanent, the institution as a whole was changed, and with it much else. I doubt that any of the well-meaning reformers of the 1960s predicted this. Their intention had been a noble one. They wanted to help people stuck in wretched marriages, and to lift the stigma attached to those who got divorced. But the problem of normal distribution interceded. The change didn't just affect those people. It made married people at all levels of happiness more likely to get divorced.

My money, my choice

Divorce reforms were not solely responsible for the death of marriage, of course. There were many factors. Lawmakers loosened the limits on divorce because the institution of marriage was already starting to stumble. Their reforms acted as a final shove.

The most important of these material changes was the invention of the contraceptive pill. This very clearly shows that new technologies can have very unpredictable consequences. The introduction of the Pill led to an *increase* in the number of out-of-wedlock births, rather than a decrease. This seems odd. Why?

Marriage is good

It was because the Pill ended the taboo on pre-marital sex, while not actually providing complete protection from pregnancy. It still doesn't, even though it remains the most popular method in the UK and the US.[15] With perfect use, the combined contraceptive pill is 99 per cent effective, but with typical use it is 91 per cent effective. This means that around nine in one hundred women taking it will get pregnant in a year.[16] Across a population, that is a huge number of unwanted babies.

The decriminalisation of abortion across the Western world, which arrived shortly after the introduction of the Pill, provided a 'backup' option in these cases. In the USA, about half of women who have abortions report that they were using contraception when they became pregnant,[17] and about a quarter of all pregnancies end in abortion. For a married woman who can cope with an 'oops' baby, the Pill is a good option. But for everyone else, it doesn't actually deliver what it's supposed to.

And yet it was effective enough to dramatically change social norms. A journalist who was young when the Pill was introduced reflected in later life on this:

> It often seemed more polite to sleep with a man than to chuck him out of your flat.
>
> True, we'd been brought up to say 'no' to sex, but the only reason for that was because we might get pregnant . . . But now, armed with the pill, and with every man knowing you were armed with the pill, pregnancy was no longer a reason to say 'no' to sex.

Marriage is good

And men exploited this mercilessly. Now, for them, 'no' always meant 'yes'.[18]

From the 1970s onwards, it became much less common for women to wait until marriage or engagement before having sex. And, while in theory *the choice* to refuse pre-marital sex still existed, in practice it became a much harder option to stick with. Remaining a virgin for long is now stigmatised, for both men and women.[19]

So the sexual revolution meant that motherhood became a biological choice for women in a way that it had never been before. As a result, fatherhood became a social choice for men. Or, as the comedian Dave Chappelle has put it (in jest, but describing a very real attitude):

Not only do [women] have the right to choose, I don't believe they should have to consult anybody except for a physician . . . Gentleman, that is fair. But ladies, to be fair to us, if you decide to have the baby, the man should not have to pay . . . My money, my choice.[20]

Plenty of modern men seem to agree with Chappelle. Before the death of marriage, only the most flagrant scoundrel would refuse to acknowledge and support his children if he was in a publicly recognised relationship with their mother at the time of conception. Now, deadbeat dads are commonplace. In the UK, fewer than two-thirds of parents who don't live with their children – almost all of them

Marriage is good

fathers – are paying child support in full.[21] In America, the figure is less than half.[22] Not only are record numbers of children not growing up with a father at home, but many of those children don't even get any money out of these absent men.

Despite the often valiant efforts of single mothers, the data clearly show that, on average, children without fathers at home do not do as well as other children.[23] Fatherlessness is associated with higher incarceration rates for boys,[24] higher rates of teen pregnancy for girls,[25] and a greater likelihood of emotional and behavioural problems for both sexes.[26] This is not only because children are denied the material support their fathers might have given them. It's also because single mothers have the almost impossible task of doing everything themselves. They have to earn all of the money as well as looking after their children.

Then there are stepparents. This mostly means step-fathers, as mothers usually gain custody of children and so children mostly interact with stepfathers. Unfortunately, child abuse is far more commonly committed by step-parents than biological parents. This is known as 'the Cinderella effect'. Psychologist Steven Pinker has described stepparenthood as 'the strongest risk factor for child abuse ever identified'. A stepparent is forty to one hundred times more likely than a biological parent to kill a child.[27] Stepfathers are also far more likely than genetic fathers to sexually abuse children.

Stepchildren, on average, have a tough time of it. They find home life more stressful than other children do. They

Marriage is good

leave home younger, often due to family conflict. They suffer more stress, are more likely to die young, they get fed less, and even tend to be shorter. All of this holds true across cultures.[28]

Of course, it is sometimes better for children not to live with their genetic fathers, or even have contact with them, particularly if those men are dangerous. And, of course, there are plenty of stepparents that do a great job. The presence of a stepparent in a young child's home does not guarantee that the child will do worse. But it does make it more likely.

So, parents are kidding themselves if they think that a divorce or separation will have no impact on their children. And, as is often the case, it is poor women who fare worst. Divorce almost always means a reduction in income for the mother (and the child, who probably lives with her). This means moving to poorer quality housing, less time for leisure, and so on.[29]

And the situation is even worse for mothers who were never married in the first place. A recent BBC documentary about homeless single mothers included an interview with the father of one of the toddlers featured in the programme. Both child and mother were living in a hostel run by the local council, heavily in debt, and surviving on benefits. She desperately wanted to get back with her ex. He would occasionally swing by the hostel to spend time with their son, making vague promises about them one day living together as a family. Addressing the camera, he explained his view of the situation:

Marriage is good

> It's always good to spend time with my kid. I wish that I could see him when I want to see him, but I think sometimes you have to prioritise your lifestyle.[30]

This man was not willing to make even the most minor sacrifice in order to offer his child and ex-girlfriend a stable homelife. And why should he? From his perspective, *she* was the one who had decided not to have an abortion, and so *she* must face the consequences alone. Which means that she became dependent on the state. My friend Mason Hartman compares the modern state to a kind of 'back-up husband'. If called upon, it will feed you, house you, and protect you from violence, but it won't do so especially well. And the state will offer no warmth or companionship alongside these basic necessities.

I don't suggest for a moment that this 'back-up husband' ought now to withdraw. If the welfare state were to disappear, the result would be misery and mayhem for the most vulnerable members of our society. But nor do I think that the 'back-up husband' is anything like as good as the real thing. It turns out that marriage served an important purpose. It helped protect the interests of both women and, crucially, children. Despite all our efforts, feminists have not yet found a workable alternative.

A baby and someone

Many feminists consider the death of marriage to be a good thing. 'The institution of marriage is the chief vehicle for the perpetuation of the oppression of women', insisted the

Marriage is good

American sociologist Marlene Dixon in 1969, summarising the dominant feminist view of the time.[31]

However, it's no coincidence that most of the feminists who opposed marriage never had children. If you value freedom above all else, then you must reject motherhood. Being a mother limits a woman's freedom in almost every possible way, for her whole life. She will always have obligations to her children, and they will always have obligations to her. It's a connection that is only ever broken in the most dire circumstances.

Feminists have historically challenged this restriction on freedom through advocating greater availability of contraception and abortion. This has been effective up to a point. It has allowed women more of a say in when or if they have children. But what about when the children are actually born?

The fact is that feminism has a blind spot when it comes to motherhood. It has shut mothers out. That's important, given that at least three-quarters of women become mothers. Motherhood is discussed in fewer than three per cent of papers, journal articles, or textbooks on modern gender theory.[32] This is perhaps unsurprising, considering that fewer than half of female academics have children.[33] The whole topic has slipped out of sight.

And no wonder, since the logic of individualism collapses upon contact with motherhood. The pregnant woman's frame contains two people, neither of them truly autonomous. The unborn baby depends on the mother for survival, and the mother cannot break this physical bond

Marriage is good

except through medical intervention that will result in the baby's death. Even after birth, the mother–baby duo remains closely tied together. Babies and young children won't survive without the devoted care of at least one parent, usually the mother. As the famous child psychologist Donald Winnicott has written, 'there is no such thing as a baby. There is only a baby and someone.'

Some feminists insist that women ought to forego motherhood altogether – if women cannot participate in reproduction and remain autonomous, these critics argue, then they should not participate at all. This does work up to a point – for the individual, at least, if not for the species. But it isn't possible to remain autonomous, even if a woman chooses never to have children. She will one day grow old, and depend on other people as if she were an infant all over again.

A modified version of Winnicott's proclamation could be applied to almost all adults at some stage of their lives: 'there is no such thing as a person. There is only a person and someone.' Acting as that 'someone' means giving away some of your freedom, which runs against what we're all supposed to want. Many feminists of the second wave described their goal as 'women's liberation' – womankind was in chains, they said, and those chains had to be broken. And that goal was understandable, given that women are still too often always caring but never cared for.

But the solution to this problem cannot be individualism, because the whole concept is based on a lie. We all begin as dependent babies, spend a very brief period as

Marriage is good

relatively independent young adults, before caring for our own dependent children, and then ultimately ending our lives in what Shakespeare called our 'second childishness'.[34] Modern contraception has allowed us to extend young adult stage, giving the illusion that independence is our permanent state. But it isn't – it's nothing more than a blip, which some of us will never experience at all. So, we have to find a way of being dependent upon one another.

The protection of marriage

Dependency, nevertheless, continues to present problems for feminism, particularly in relation to motherhood. The only help for mothers in which modern feminists are usually interested is state help. They want the state – the 'backup husband' – to provide childcare in the form of 24/7 daycare centres. This is efficient, since, instead of one mother devoted to one child, the backup husband allocates one worker to many children. Mothers can thus return promptly to work and put their tax revenue towards funding this childcare system.

Such a model depends on physically prising women apart from their children, making them both as autonomous as possible, as quickly as possible. In a way, this increases women's freedom. However, it doesn't give women a way of being physically *with* their children, while also being materially and emotionally supported by other adults. Many feminists see marriage as a method used by men to control female sexuality. And it does do that, of course, but

Marriage is good

that was never its sole function. There is another one. To protect children.

The faithless soldier

Marriage used to be defined as 'a holy mystery in which man and woman become one flesh' – and therefore produce children. There were always exceptions to this – infertile people were permitted to marry, as were people beyond reproductive age. Nonetheless, marriage was understood to be based around the idea of two sexually complementary people whose union 'would naturally be fulfilled by . . . their having and rearing children together'.[35]

For most Westerners, this is no longer what marriage means. The psychologist Eli Finkel argues that there have been different stages in how we understand marriage, related to economics.[36] Before the mid-nineteenth century, surviving day to day was often a struggle, so what most people wanted in a spouse was help with the basics: food, shelter, etc. Later, as most people got richer, couples had the luxury of placing more emphasis on love in their marriages. Then, in the affluent 1960s, we entered an era in which self-discovery, self-esteem and personal growth became the key markers of a marriage's success.

Where once marriage was all about babies and pooling resources, it is now usually understood as a means of sexual and emotional fulfilment. Since the old meaning of marriage is now forgotten, it makes sense to give same sex couples, who necessarily cannot have biological children, the right to marry. But we should not make the mistake

Marriage is good

of misrepresenting the historical purpose of marriage and the prohibition on pre-marital sex. Modern feminists easily forget that, before contraception, prohibiting sex before marriage served *female* interests, not male. It protected the group of people who bear (literally) the consequences of extramarital pregnancy.

This point was well understood by feminists who were born long before the Pill. They knew what an extramarital pregnancy meant for a woman in a society without a welfare state. Yes, it's true that part of the harm was done by stigma: single mothers were outcasts. But the biggest catastrophe was *single motherhood itself.* It could result, for some poor women, in the following: prostitution, starvation, a dangerous attempt at abortion, abandonment of a child to an orphanage, or infanticide.

So, the stigma around single motherhood caused a great deal of misery for its many victims. It also existed for a purpose: to deter women from making an irreparable mistake for the sake of a worthless man. We might think that this is now a thing of the past. Surely that purpose is now somewhat anachronistic in an age of contraception? Maybe, but only somewhat. Illicit affairs *do still* end in trauma and tragedy because sex *is still* just as consequential as it ever was.

Many feminists who lived before the 1960s knew this better than we do now. They realised the grim consequences of sexual freedom for women. Their conclusion was that male desire needed to be constrained. This is why one of the founders of feminism, Mary Wollstonecraft, devoted a substantial chunk of her most famous book to bemoaning

Marriage is good

the lack of sexual restraint in men. They were the sex with the higher sex drive, and thus – to Wollstonecraft's mind – the greater responsibility for containing their passions. 'Votes for women, chastity for men' was a real old feminist slogan, now forgotten.[37]

The reinvention of marriage

But how to persuade men into sexual restraint? I've written earlier in this book about what I've called the 'cad' and 'dad' versions of male sexuality, with the former orientated towards casual sex, and the latter towards commitment.

Having almost reached the end of this book, I hope I've managed to persuade you that the cad mode of male sexuality is bad for women overall. The vast majority of women find it difficult to detach emotion from sex, meaning that an encounter with a cad who doesn't call is likely to leave a woman feeling distressed, even if she attempts to repress those feelings. Women did not evolve to treat sex as meaningless, and trying to pretend otherwise does not end well.

Then there are the physical consequences of sex. The danger and pain of an unwanted pregnancy are experienced solely by the woman. Modern forms of contraception are mostly effective, but they still regularly fail. And whatever you think about the issue more broadly, we should all be able to agree that an abortion is not a good thing for a woman. It carries medical risks like uterine damage or sepsis, and the emotional consequences are not trivial.

All in all, attempting to mimic the cad mode of male sexuality has not freed women. The Hugh Hefners of the world

Marriage is good

are not threatened by 'sexually liberated' women. Quite the opposite, in fact. They are delighted to find themselves with a buffet of young women to feast on, all of them apparently willing to suffer mistreatment without complaint.

I can't help but agree with the dark pronouncement my grandmother made when I told her about the thesis of this book: 'women have been conned'.

The task for practically minded feminists, then, is to deter men from cad mode. Our current sexual culture does not do that, but it could. To do this, we need something that discourages short-termism in male sexual behaviour, protects the economic interests of mothers, and creates a stable environment for the raising of children. And we do already have such a thing, even if it is old, clunky, and prone to regular failure. It's called monogamous marriage.

However, it's important to be clear. Lifelong monogamy is not our natural state. Only about fifteen per cent of the societies that we know of have been monogamous.[38] Monogamy has to be enforced through laws and customs. Even within societies in which it is the norm, plenty of people are defiant.

To date, monogamy has been dominant in only two types of society. There are small-scale groups beset by serious environmental problems, and some of the most complex civilisations to have ever existed, including our own.[39] Almost all others have been polygynous, permitting high-status men to take multiple wives. Indeed, large and unequal societies like our own tend to revert back to polygyny when the societal expectation of strict monogamy is removed.

Marriage is good

But, while the monogamous marriage model may be relatively unusual, it is also spectacularly successful. When monogamy is imposed on a society, it tends to become richer. It has lower rates of both child abuse and domestic violence, since conflict between co-wives tends to generate both. Birth rates and crime rates both fall, which encourages economic development. Wealthy men, denied the opportunity to devote their resources to acquiring more wives, instead invest elsewhere: in property, businesses, employees and other productive endeavours.

This is, it seems, the solution to what anthropologists have called 'the puzzle of monogamous marriage'. How is it that a marriage system that does not suit the interests of the most powerful members of society – high-status men – has nevertheless come to be dominant in much of the world? The answer is that, although monogamy is less satisfactory for these men, it produces wealthy, stable societies that survive.

A monogamous marriage system is successful in part because it pushes men away from cad mode, particularly when premarital sex is also prohibited. Under these circumstances, if a man wants to have sex in a way that's socially acceptable, he has to make himself marriageable. This means holding down a good job and setting up a household suitable for the raising of children. He has to tame himself, in other words.

Fatherhood then has a further taming effect, even at the biochemical level: when men are involved in the care of their young children, their testosterone levels drop, along-

Marriage is good

side their aggression and sex drive.[40] A society composed of tamed men is a better society to live in, for men, for women, and for children.

Monogamous marriage is also the best solution yet discovered to the problems presented by childrearing. The traditional solution was that the father was mainly responsible for earning money while the mother was mainly responsible for caring for children at home. There was wisdom to this. It allows mothers and children to be physically together and at the same time financially supported.

In an age of labour-saving devices like washing machines, it has become less time-consuming to run a household. This has made it possible for mothers of young children to do paid work outside the home, as most of us do. But attempting to play the traditional roles of mother and father simultaneously – as single mothers are forced to – is close to impossible. For some women, paid work outside the home is a joy and a privilege. For many more, it is a responsibility, and often an onerous one. Even those women who enjoy their work are physically unable to perform it during the early months of a baby's life.

I should know: I began this book at the beginning of my pregnancy, and completed it when my son was six months old. Writing is probably one of the easiest jobs to combine with motherhood but, even so, there were weeks on end during which I didn't write a word because I was too busy caring for my baby. And, while I could be practically supported by other people, including my husband, I was irreplaceable as mother. This is not only because I

Marriage is good

was the only person who could breastfeed. It's also because children have a relationship with their mothers that starts from conception, and that relationship cannot be handed over to another without distress to both mother and baby.

If we want to keep that maternal bond intact, then the only solution is for another person to step in during these times of vulnerability and do the tasks needed to keep a household warm and fed. Perhaps we could call that person a spouse. Perhaps we could call their legal and emotional bond a marriage.

I have just one piece of advice to offer in this chapter, and you've probably already guessed what it will be. So, here it is: get married. And do your best to stay married. Particularly if you have children, and particularly if those children are still young. And if you do find yourself in the position of being a single mother, wait until your children are older before you bring a stepfather into their home. This advice is harder to follow now than it used to be, because we no longer live in a society that encourages staying married. But it is still possible for individuals to go against the grain, and insist on doing the harder, less fashionable thing.

The critics of marriage are right to say that it has historically been used by men to control women. They're also right to point out that most marriages do not live up to a romantic ideal. They're right, too, that monogamous, lifelong marriage is in a sense 'unnatural', in that it is not the human norm. The marriage system that prevailed in the

Marriage is good

West up until recently was not perfect. It wasn't easy for most people, since it demanded high levels of tolerance and self-control. Where the critics go wrong is in arguing that there is any better system. There isn't.

Conclusion

LISTEN TO YOUR MOTHER

I'm treading a fine line in this book. On the one hand, I'm arguing that it's hard to make completely free choices in the society we live in. On the other hand, I'm trying to encourage readers to make particular choices. In other words, I'm telling you that your options are limited, but that you do still have them. 'There are ways out', as the poet Charles Bukowski puts it, 'there is light somewhere, it may not be much light, but it beats the darkness.'

So, I've tried to offer chinks of light. Because I truly believe, not only that there is scope for individuals to behave differently, but also that these individual actions can add up to something more significant. Things can change very quickly when people realise that there are others who secretly feel the same way as they do.

My friend, the writer Katherine Dee, has been predicting a change for some time. Her predictions are often spot on.

Listen to Your Mother

She observes more and more signs of a coming reaction against the excesses of sexual liberation, particular from Gen Z women who have experienced the worst of it.[1] I think Katherine is right. They have been utterly failed by liberal feminism. They have the most to gain from a swing back against its excesses.

So, while there is advice within these pages that could be helpful to any reader, it is worth repeating here the points that are most relevant to these particular young women. This is the same advice I would offer my own daughter:

- Distrust anything that puts pressure on you to ignore your moral instincts.
- Chivalry is actually a good thing. We all have to control our sexual desires, and men particularly so, given their greater physical strength and average higher sex drives.
- Sometimes (though not always) you can readily spot sexually aggressive men. There are usually impulsive, sleep around, ultra-macho and selfish. Be wary around men like this.
- A man who is aroused by violence is a man to avoid, whether or not he uses BDSM to excuse his behaviour. If he can maintain an erection while beating a woman, he isn't safe to be alone with.
- Consent workshops are mostly useless. The best way of reducing rape is by reducing the opportunities for would-be rapists to offend. This can be done either by keeping convicted rapists in prison, or by limiting their access to potential victims.

Conclusion

- The category of people most likely to become victims of these men are young women aged about thirteen to twenty-five. All girls and women, but particularly those in this age category, should avoid being alone with men they don't know, or men who give them the creeps. Gut instinct is not to be ignored: it's usually triggered by a red flag that's well worth noticing.
- Get drunk or high in private and with female friends rather than in public or in mixed company.
- Don't use dating apps. Mutual friends can vet histories and punish bad behaviour. Dating apps can't.
- Holding off having sex with a new boyfriend for at least a few months is a good way of discovering whether or not he's serious about you, or just looking for a hook-up.
- Only have sex with a man if you think he would make a good father to your children. This isn't because you necessarily intend to have children with him, but because this is a good rule of thumb in deciding whether or not he's worthy of your trust.
- Monogamous marriage is by far the most stable and reliable foundation on which to build a family.

I wrote in the first chapter that none of my advice would be ground breaking, and I stand by that. It is all based on scientific research, but it shouldn't have to be, since this is pretty much what most mothers would tell their daughters, if only they were willing to listen.

There is no need to reinvent the wheel. We have to look at social structures that have already proven to be success-

Listen to Your Mother

ful in the past. There is no point in basing our hopes on some imagined alternative that has never existed and is never likely to. The technology shock of the Pill led liberals to think that our society could be uniquely free from having sexual rules that constrain us. The last sixty years have proved this idea to be wrong. We need to re-erect the social safeguards that have been torn down. And, in order to do that, we have to start by stating the obvious. Sex must be taken seriously. Men and women are different. Not all desires are good. Consent is not enough. Violence is not love. Loveless sex is not empowering. People are not products. Marriage is good. Above all, listen to your mother.

In 2021, a TikTok video by a young American woman called Abby went viral online. In the video, Abby tells the camera:

> I, like many other college students, am someone who is entangled in hook-up culture, and often hook-up culture makes it difficult for me to determine whether or not what I'm doing is good for me and kind to myself. Very often as women we are led astray from what we actually deserve. So here's what I've been doing lately . . .

She pulls up on screen a series of childhood photos of herself, and explains that the men she's hooked up with in the past have often made her feel as though she's undeserving, not only of love, but also basic respect. So, she's trying to remind herself of her worth as a person by playing the

143

Conclusion

role of mother to her inner child. 'Am I ok with that for her?' she asks tearfully, gesturing at her younger self in the photo. 'Would I let her be a late night, drunk second option? Would I let this happen to her?' She shakes her head, weeping: 'From a third person, caretaker point of view, I would never let any of this stuff happen to her.'[2]

Abby is trying to mother herself, though she isn't quite sure how to do it. And the thousands of young women in her replies are trying to do the same ('I'm sobbing', 'I really needed this, thank you', 'This just changed my life'). They've been denied the guidance of mothers, not because their actual mothers are unwilling to offer it, but modern feminism has encouraged them not to listen. This means not only that they are cut off from the voices of experience, but – more importantly – they are also cut off from the person who loves them most in the world. Feminism needs to rediscover the mother, in every sense.

Until we do, each individual woman will have to learn on her own the lie of the promise of sexual freedom. It was a lie all along. It's time, at last, to say so.

NOTES

1 Sex must be taken seriously

1 Gianluca Mezzofiore, 'No, that viral picture doesn't show Hugh Hefner lighting a cigarette for Marilyn Monroe', 28 September 2017, https://mashable.com/article/marilyn-monroe-hugh-hefner-fake-picture-playboy.

2 Jack Shepherd, 'Hugh Hefner dead: Playboy founder is being buried next to Marilyn Monroe', 28 September 2017, https://www.independent.co.uk/arts-entertainment/films/news/hugh-hefner-is-being-buried-in-a-plot-next-to-marilyn-monroe-a7971311.html.

3 Jeff Gottlieb, 'For sale: eternity with Marilyn Monroe', 14 August 2009, www.latimes.com/archives/la-xpm-2009-aug-14-me-marilyn14-story.html.

4 Brad Witter, 'Marilyn Monroe didn't actually pose

Notes to pp. 2–14

for the first issue of *Playboy*', 8 September 2020, https://www.biography.com/actors/marilyn-monroe-playboy-first-issue-didnt-pose.

5 'Hugh Hefner will be buried next to Marilyn Monroe', 29 September 2017, www.telegraph.co.uk/films/2017/09/29/hugh-hefner-buried-next-marilyn-monroe-fans-not-happy/.

6 Megan C. Hills, 'How Hugh Hefner built an entire empire without Marilyn Monroe's consent', 29 September 2017, www.marieclaire.co.uk/news/celebrity-news/hugh-hefner-marilyn-mon roe-541688.

7 'Remembering Hugh Hefner through his sharpest, funniest quotes', 28 September 2017, https://ew.com/news/2017/09/28/hugh-hefner-quotes/.

8 Brooks Barnes, 'The loin in winter', 23 October 2009, https://www.nytimes.com/2009/10/24/business/media/24hefner.html.

9 See https://www.theguardian.com/film/2017/mar/05/emma-watson-vanity-fair-cover-feminism.

10 https://medium.com/@totalsratmove/is-it-possible-that-there-is-something-in-between-consensual-sex-and-rape-and-that-it-happens-to-2194a96bdbb6.

11 C. S. Lewis, *Surprised by Joy*. London: Geoffrey Bles, 1955, p. 207.

12 Laura House, 'Plan dinner the night before, NEVER complain and speak in a soft voice', 7 December 2016, https://www.dailymail.co.uk/femail/article-4011366/Cringeworthy-1950s-marriage-advice-teaching-house wives-look-husbands.html.

Notes to pp. 14–22

13 https://www.cosmopolitan.com/sex-love/advice/g3765/ways-to-please-a-man/.

14 https://www.cosmopolitan.com/uk/love-sex/sex/tips/g1508/turn-him-on-sex-tips/.

15 https://www.cosmopolitan.com/sex-love/confessions/advice/g1788/how-to-turn-him-on/.

16 https://www.cosmopolitan.com/sex-love/news/a41845/worst-things-playmates-said-about-playboy-mansion/.

17 https://www.thewrap.com/hugh-hefner-legacy-no-feminist-hero/; https://www.thesun.co.uk/news/4585472/brit-model-lured-girls-to-the-playboy-mansion-to-have-orgies-with-hugh-hefner/.

2 Men and women are different

1 Randy Thornhill and Craig T. Palmer, *A Natural History of Rape: Biological Bases of Sexual Coercion*. Chicago: MIT Press, 2000.

2 Alice Dreger, *Galileo's Middle Finger: Heretics, Activists, and One Scholar's Search for Justice*. New York: Penguin, p. 124.

3 Susan Brownmiller, *Against Our Will: Men, Women and Rape*. New York: Simon & Schuster, 1975, p. 6 [Kindle location 199].

4 A. E. Miller, J. D. MacDougall, M. A. Tarnopolsky and D. G. Sale, 'Gender differences in strength and muscle fiber characteristics', *European Journal of Applied Physiology and Occupational Physiology* 66 (1993): 254–62.

5 Paul Gabrielsen, 'Why males pack a powerful punch',

Notes to pp. 22–31

5 February 2020, https://phys.org/news/2020-02-males-powerful.html.

6 D. Leyk, W. Gorges, D. Ridder et al., 'Hand-grip strength of young men, women and highly trained female athletes', *European Journal of Applied Physiology* 99 (2007): 415–21.

7 Robinson Meyer, 7 August 2012, https://www.theatlantic.com/technology/archive/2012/08/the-golden-ratio-the-one-number-that-describes-how-mens-world-records-compare-with-womens/260758/.

8 See https://en.wikipedia.org/wiki/CARIFTA_Games #Boys_Under_17.

9 See https://www.youtube.com/watch?v=wTHgMxQ EoPI.

10 Richard B. Felson and Patrick R. Cundiff, 'Sexual assault as a crime against young people', *Archives of Sexual Behavior* 43 (2014): 273–84.

11 Thornhill and Palmer, *A Natural History of Rape*, p. 72.

12 Richard Felson and Richard Moran, 2 January 2016, https://quillette.com/2016/01/02/to-rape-is-to-want-sex -not-power/.

13 T. A. Gannon, R. M. Collie, T. Ward and J. Thakker, 'Rape: Psychopathology, theory and treatment', *Clinical Psychology Review* 28 (2008): 982–1008.

14 Thornhill and Palmer, *A Natural History of Rape*, p. 134.

15 Dreger, *Galileo's Middle Finger*, pp. 118–20.

16 David Buss, *The Evolution of Desire: Strategies of Human Mating*. New York: Basic Books, [1994] 2016, p. 256.

17 'Sussex Police defends 'victim blaming' campaign poster',

Notes to pp. 32–43

8 April 2015, www.bbc.co.uk/news/uk-england-sussex-32216176.

18 See www.change.org/p/sussex-police-withdraw-your-rape-prevention-posters-which-blames-victims-of-sexual-assault.

3 Not all desires are good

1 David P. Schmitt, 'Sociosexuality from Argentina to Zimbabwe: A 48-nation study of sex, culture, and strategies of human mating', *Behavioral and Brain Sciences* 28 (2005): 247–75; discussion, 275–311.

2 See https://www.bsa.natcen.ac.uk/latest-report/british-social-attitudes-30/personal-relationships/homosexuality.aspx.

3 See https://en.wikipedia.org/wiki/Legal_status_of_same-sex_marriage.

4 G.K. Chesterton, *The Thing: Why I Am a Catholic*. London: Sheed & Ward, 1929, ch. 4.

5 Geoffrey Robertson, 24 May 2008, https://www.thetimes.com/article/the-mary-whitehouse-story-mary-quite-contrary-dgqdtrf2qxq.

6 Daniel Boffey, 'Revealed: how Jimmy Savile abused up to 1,000 victims on BBC premises', 18 January 2014, https://www.theguardian.com/media/2014/jan/18/jimmy-savile-abused-1000-victims-bbc.

7 Louis Theroux, 'Looking back on Jimmy Savile', 1 October 2016, www.bbc.co.uk/news/magazine-37517619.

8 Scott D'Arcy and Dan Bloom, 'Paedophile Information

Notes to pp. 44–57

Exchange: Leon Brittan "opposed banning pro-child sex campaign group'", 4 June 2015, https://www.mirror. co.uk/news/uk-news/paedophile-information-exchange-leon-brittan-5825108.

9 Tim Stanley, 1 March 2014, https://web.archive.org/web /20140306014809/http://blogs.telegraph.co.uk/news /timstanley/100261734/allen-ginsberg-camille-paglia-and-the-literary-champions-of-paedophilia/.

10 See https://en.wikipedia.org/wiki/Color_Climax_Corp oration.

11 See https://twitter.com/RepJimBanks/status/130455652 5789351937.

12 See www.telegraph.co.uk/films/0/cuties-netflix-reviewa -provocative-powder-keg-age-terrified/.

13 Francesca Bacardi, 14 January 2021, https://pagesix. com/2021/01/14/armie-hammers-ex-courtney-vuce kovich-he-wanted-to-barbecue-and-eat-me/; Mike Vulpo, 26 January 2021, www.eonline.com/news/1231009/armie-hammers-ex-paige-lorenze-details-their-polyamorous-bdsm-relationship.

14 Katie Way, 'I went on a date with Aziz Ansari', https:// babe.net/2018/01/13/aziz-ansari-28355.

4 Loveless sex is not empowering

1 Karley Sciortino, *Slutever: Dispatches from a Sexually Autonomous Woman in a Post-Shame World.* New York: Grand Central, 2018, pp. 10–11

2 'The revised sociosexual orientation inventory (SOI-

Notes to pp. 58–62

    R) short manual', www.larspenke.eu/pdfs/SOI-R%20 Manual.pdf.

3 David P. Schmitt, 'Sociosexuality from Argentina to Zimbabwe: a 48-nation study of sex, culture, and strategies of human mating', *Behavioral and Brain Sciences* 28 (2005): 247–75; discussion, 275–311.

4 R. D. Clark and E. Hatfield, 'Gender differences in receptivity to sexual offers', *Journal of Psychology & Human Sexuality* 2 (1989): 39–55.

5 Al-Shawaf, D. M. Lewis and D. M. Buss, 'Sex differences in disgust: why are women more easily disgusted than men?', *Emotion Review* 10 (2018): 149–60.

6 Diane M. Kedzierski, *An Examination of Disgust, its Measures, and Gender Differences in the Experience of Disgust Sensitivity.* PhD dissertation, Nova Southeastern University, Florida, 2013; https://nsuworks.nova.edu/cps_stuetd/43.

7 Rachel Moran, *Paid For: My Journey through Prostitution.* Dublin: Gill & Macmillan, 2013.

8 See https://everydayfeminism.com/2016/07/feminist-hook-up-culture/ and https://www.mic.com/articles/57795/your-7-point-intersectional-feminist-guide-to-hook-ups.

9 https://www.elle.com/uk/life-and-culture/culture/a32765/what-it-means-to-be-demisexual/.

10 See www.womenshealthmag.com/relationships/a30224236/casual-sex-feelings/; https://www.vice.com/en/article/59mmzq/how-to-bio-hack-your-brain-to-have-sex-without-getting-emotionally-attached?utm_source=vicefbus;

Notes to pp. 63–67

https://elle.in/article/how-to-have-casual-sex-without-getting-emotionally-attached-according-to-science/.

11 Justin R. Garcia et al., 'Sexual hookup culture: A review', *Review of General Psychology* 16 (2012): 161–76.

12 Lisa Wade, 'The rise of hookup culture on American college campuses', 25 August 2017, https://scholars.org/brief/rise-hookup-sexual-culture-american-college-campuses.

13 Leah Fessler, 'A lot of women don't enjoy hookup culture – so why do we force ourselves to participate?', 17 May 2016, https://qz.com/685852/hookup-culture/.

14 R. L. Fielder and M. P. Carey, 'Prevalence and characteristics of sexual hookups among first-semester female college students', *Journal of Sex & Marital Therapy* 36 (2010): 346–59.

15 E. A. Armstrong, P. England and A. C. K. Fogarty, 'Accounting for women's orgasm and sexual enjoyment in college hookups and relationships', *American Sociological Review* 77 (2012): 435–62.

16 David Buss and David Schmitt, 'Sexual strategies theory: an evolutionary perspective on human mating', *Psychological Review* 100 (1993): 204–32.

17 David Buss, *The Evolution of Desire: Strategies of Human Mating*. New York: Basic Books, [1994] 2016, p. 137.

18 Sherry Argov, *Why Men Love Bitches*. New York: Adams Media, p. 55.

19 Donald E. Brown, Human Universals. New York: McGraw-Hill, 1991.

20 Derek A. Kreager and Jeremy Staff, 'The sexual double

Notes to pp. 67–78

standard and adolescent peer acceptance', Social *Psychology Quarterly* 72 (2009): 143–64.

21 Michael J. Marks, Tara M. Young and Yuliana Zaikman, 'The sexual double standard in the real world', *Social Psychology* 50 (2019): 67–79.

22 Daniel N. Jones, 'The 'chasing Amy' bias in past sexual experiences: men can change, women cannot', *Sexuality & Culture* 20 (2016): 24–37.

23 See https://www.reddit.com/r/relationships/comments/72115r/i25m_told_my_friends_with_benefits24f_i_dont_see/.

24 Yanna J. Weisberg, Colin G. DeYoung and Jacob B. Hirsh, 'Gender differences in personality across the ten aspects of the Big Five', *Frontiers in Psychology* 2 (2011): 178; doi: 10.3389/fpsyg .2011.00178.

5 Consent is not enough

1 See https://www.stylist.co.uk/people/10-unlikely-oxford-union-speakers/13301.

2 See https://filmdaily.co/news/jenna-jameson-porn-traffic king/.

3 See https://web.archive.org/web/20141219160919/http://www.slate.com/articles/technology/technology/2014/10/mindgeek_porn_monopoly_its_dominance_is_a_cautionary_tale_for_other_industries.html.

4 See https://www.nytimes.com/2020/12/09/opinion/pornhub-news-child-abuse.html.

5 See https://www.theguardian.com/technology/2020

Notes to pp. 79–83

/dec/14/pornhub-purge-removes-unverified-videos-investigation-child-abuse.

6 See https://www.10news.com/news/local-news/women-sue-pornhubs-parent-company-for-hosting-girlsdoporn-com-videos.

7 See https://timesofsandiego.com/crime/2021/04/02/10-more-women-join-lawsuit-against-pornhub-plaintiffs-now-total-50/.

8 T. Jacobs, K. Fog-Poulsen, A. Vermandel et al., 'The effect of porn watching on erectile function', *European Urology Open Science* 19, Supplement e1121–e1122, July 2020.

9 See https://www.mirashowers.co.uk/blog/trends/revealed-what-brits-are-really-getting-up-to-in-the-bathroom.

10 See https://www.bbc.co.uk/bbcthree/article/bb79a2ce-0de4-4965-98f0-9ebbcfcc2a60.

11 Charmaine Borg and Peter J. de Jong, 'Feelings of disgust and disgust-induced avoidance weaken following induced sexual arousal in women', *PLoS ONE* 7 (2012): e44111.

12 C.-E. Ivan, 'On disgust and moral judgments: A review', *Journal of European Psychology Students* 6 (2015): 25–36.

13 See https://quillette.com/2019/05/31/how-limbic-capitalism-preys-on-our-addicted-brains/.

14 Darryl T. Gwynne and David C. F. Rentz, 'Beetles on the bottle: male buprestids mistake stubbies for females (Coleoptera)', *Australian Journal of Entomology* 22 (1983): 79–80.

15 See https://www.theguardian.com/lifeandstyle/2019/mar/11/young-men-porn-induced-erectile-dysfunction.

Notes to pp. 83–95

16 See https://edition.cnn.com/2016/02/24/entertainment/terry-crews-porn-addition-feat/index.html.

17 See https://unherd.com/2020/06/why-doesnt-porn-ever-get-cancelled/.

6 Violence is not love

1 Theodore Dalrymple, *Life at the Bottom: The Worldview that Makes the Underclass*. Chicago: Ivan R. Dee, 2001, pp. 75–6.

2 Ibid., p. 78.

3 Andreas Wismeijer and Marcel van Assen, 'Psychological characteristics of BDSM practitioners', *Journal of Sexual Medicine* 10 (2013): 1943–52.

4 Roxane Gay, *Bad Feminist*. New York: HarperCollins, 2014, p. 184.

5 See https://www.theguardian.com/society/2020/nov/22/if-im-not-in-on-friday-i-might-be-dead-chilling-facts-about-uk-femicide.

6 See https://www.bbc.com/news/uk-50546184.

7 See https://www.menshealth.com/sex-women/a33382089/breath-play-erotic-asphyxiation-bdsm/.

8 Helen Bichard, Christopher Byrne, Christopher W. N. Saville and Rudi Coetzer, 'The neuropsychological outcomes of nonfatal strangulation in domestic and sexual violence: a systematic review', *Neuropsychological Rehabilitation*, 12 January 2021.

9 Interview with Helen Bichard, 30 July 2020.

10 https://www.dailymail.co.uk/news/article-8552589/

Notes to pp. 95–103

Businessman-killed-lover-used-rough-sex-defence-FREED-two-years.html.

11 https://www.thedailybeast.com/iranian-found-in-venice-lagoon-alleged-victim-of-botched-sex-game?account=thedailybeast&medium=twitter&source=socialflow.

12 https://www.thesun.co.uk/news/7108595/suspect-paedo-dumps-teens-body-pavement-bdsm/.

13 https://metro.co.uk/2016/05/18/psychologist-dies-after-asking-flatmate-to-strangle-her-during-sex-5889007/.

14 https://www.pnn.de/kultur/ueberregional/trauerspiel-alexander-und-natalia-ein/21848546.html.

15 https://www.independent.co.uk/news/world/americas/us-man-disembowels-woman-uttering-wrong-name-during-sex-10512965.html.

16 Rosamund Urwin and Esmé O'Keeffe, 26 January 2020, https://www.thetimes.com/business-money/technology/article/social-media-make-girls-think-choking-during-sex-is-normal-0jlrgf2b0.

17 Interview with Clare McGlynn, 29 May 2020.

18 Dolly Alderton, 18 April 2021, https://www.thetimes.com/life-style/sex-relationships/article/dear-dolly-im-a-feminist-so-why-am-i-only-attracted-to-misogynists-20cgws8z8.

7 People are not products

1 Kate Lister, 'Sex and money', in *A Curious History of Sex*. London: Unbound, 2020.

2 Rachel Moran, *Paid For: My Journey through Prostitution*.

Notes to pp. 105–108

Cork: Gill & Macmillan, 2013, pp. 112–13.

3 Julie Bindel, *The Pimping of Prostitution: Abolishing the Sex Work Myth*. Basingstoke: Palgrave Macmillan, 2017, p. 60.

4 Douglas Fox, 'Don't criminalise our clients', 19 November 2008, www.theguardian.com/profile/douglas-fox.

5 Bindel, *The Pimping of Prostitution*, p. 22.

6 Elizabeth Bernstein, 'What's wrong with prostitution? What's right with sex work? Comparing markets in female sexual labor', *Hastings Women's Law Journal* 10 (1999): 91–117.

7 See https://quillette.com/2019/11/16/thorstein-veblens -theory-of-the-leisure-class-a-status-update/.

8 S. Cunningham, T. Sanders, L. Platt et al., 'Sex work and occupational homicide: Analysis of a U.K. murder database', *Homicide Studies* 22 (2018): 321–38.

9 John J. Potterat, Devon D. Brewer, Stephen Q. Muth et al., 'Mortality in a long-term open cohort of prostitute women', *American Journal of Epidemiology* 159 (2004): 778–85.

10 Brooke Magnanti, *The Sex Myth: Why Everything We're Told Is Wrong*. London: Weidenfeld & Nicolson, 2012.

11 Tiggey May, Alex Harocopos and Michael Hough, *For Love or Money: Pimps and the Management of Sex Work*. London: Home Office, 2000.

12 S. Adriaenssens and J. Hendrickx, 'What can internet data tell about safe work? Unsafe sex and contract breach as proxies of quality of work in prostitution', COST ProsPol Action meeting, Ljubljana, 2016.

13 Ibid.

14 Aaron Sibarium, 23 September 2020, https://american compass.org/three-theses-about-cuties/.

15 Robin Hanson, 26 April 2018, https://www.overcoming bias.com/p/two-types-of-envyhtml.

16 Jordan Weissmann, 28 April 2018, https://slate.com /business/2018/04/economist-robin-hanson-might-be-americas-creepiest-professor.html.

17 Jordan Weissmann, 28 April 2018, https://slate.com /business/2018/04/economist-robin-hanson-might-be-americas-creepi est-professor.html.

18 Vednita Carter, 'The pimping of prostitution', www.youtube.com/watch?v=2Y-VmuKmsP0.

19 Arwa Mahdawi, 'The WAP uproar shows conservatives are fine with female sexuality – as long as men control it', 15 August 2020, https://www.theguardian.com/ commentisfree/2020/aug/15/cardi-b-megan-thee-stalion-wap-conservatives-female-sexuality.

20 See https://invisible-men-canada.tumblr.com.

21 Thomas Hollands, 24 April 2020, https://xsrus.com/the-economics-of-onlyfans.

22 Quoted in James Mumford, *Vexed: Ethics Beyond Political Tribes*. London: Bloomsbury Continuum, 2020, pp. 77–8.

23 See https://www.humanetech.com/app-ratings.

24 Andre Shakti, '8 very necessary sex tips from sex workers', 30 October 2015, www.cosmopolitan.com/sex-love/ news/a48407/sex-tips-from-sex-workers/.

Notes to pp. 119–122

8 Marriage is good

1 Aidan Lyon, 'Why are normal distributions normal?', *British Journal for the Philosophy of Science* 65 (2014): 621–49.

2 H. J. Eysenck and James A. Wakefield, 'Psychological factors as predictors of marital satisfaction', *Advances in Behaviour Research and Therapy* 3 (1981): 151–92.

3 Hansard, House of Lords debates, vol. 303, col. 297, 30 June 1969.

4 Gavin Thompson et al., *Olympic Britain: Social and Economic Change since the 1908 and 1948 London Games*. London: House of Commons Library, 2011.

5 Chiara Giordano, 'UK heterosexual marriage rate falls to lowest on record', 14 April 2020, www.independent.co.uk /news/uk/home-news/marriage-rate-uk-latest-figures-lowest-record-ons-a9 464706.html.

6 Births in England and Wales: summary tables, Office for National Statistics, Release date: 22 July 2020.

7 Thompson et al., *Olympic Britain*.

8 Dan Hurley, 19 April 2005, www.nytimes.com/2005/04 /19/health/divorce-rate-its-not-as-high-as-you-think .html.

9 W. Bradford Wilcox and Wendy Wang, 25 September 2017, https://ifstudies.org/blog/the-marriage-divide-how-and-why-working-class-families-are-more-fragile-today.

10 Susan B. Sorenson and Devan Spear, 'New data on intimate partner violence and intimate relationships: implications for gun laws and federal data collection', *Preventive Medicine* 107 (2018): 103–8.

Notes to pp. 122–125

11 Paul Amato and Alan Booth, *A Generation at Risk: Growing Up in an Era of Family Upheaval.* Cambridge, MA: Harvard University Press, 1997, p. 220.

12 Paula Span, 'The gray gender gap: older women are likelier to go it alone', 11 October 2016, www.nytimes.com/2016 /10/11/health/marital-status-elderly-health.html; Kyrsty Hazell, 31 January 2012, www.huffingtonpost.co.uk/2012 /01/31/divorced-men-are-twice-as-likely-to-remarry_n_ 1243472.html.

13 Sonia Frontera, 4 August 2021, https://www.divorcemag. com/blog/if-you-divorce-now-will-you-regret-your-divorce-later.

14 Betsey Stevenson, 'The impact of divorce laws on marriagespecific capital', *Journal of Labor Economics* 25 (2007): 75–94.

15 Nicola Davis and Niamh McIntyre, 7 March 2019, www .theguardian.com/uk-news/2019/mar/07/revealed-pill -still-most-popular-prescribed-contraceptive-in-england; Kimberly Daniels and Joyce C. Abma, 'Current contraception status among women aged 15–49', December 2018, https://www.cdc.gov/nchs/products/databriefs/db327. htm.

16 'How effective is contraception at preventing pregnancy?', 17 April 2020, http://www.nhs.uk/conditions/contracep tion/how-effective-contraception/.

17 See https://www.guttmacher.org/news-release/2018 /about-half-us-abortion-patients-report-using-contra ception-month-they-became.

18 Virginia Ironside, 18 January 2011, https://www.dailymail.

Notes to pp. 125–126

co.uk/home/you/article-1346813/The-flip-1960s-sexual-revolution-We-paid-price-free-love.html.

19 Nikola Komlenac, Manuel Pittl, Susanne Perkhofer et al., 'Links between virginity beliefs, negative feelings after virginity loss and sexual performance anxiety in a sample of German-speaking heterosexual-identified women and men', *Journal of Sex & Marital Therapy* 48 (2022): 1–18.

20 See https://www.youtube.com/watch?v=MoudH-RPnEE.

21 Hansard, House of Commons debates, vol. 561, col. 229, 15 April 2013.

22 Timothy Grall, 'Custodial mothers and fathers and their child support: 2015', January 2020, https://www.census.gov/content/dam/Census/library/publications/2020/demo/p60-262.pdf.

23 Sara McLanahan and Gary D. Sandefur, *Growing Up with a Single Parent: What Hurts, What Helps*. Cambridge, MA: Harvard University Press, 1994, p. 1.

24 Cynthia C. Harper and Sara S. McLanahan, 'Father absence and youth incarceration', *Journal of Research on Adolescence* 14 (2004): 369–97.

25 McLanahan and Sandefur, *Growing Up with a Single Parent*.

26 Nicholas Zill and Charlotte A. Schoenborn, *Developmental, Learning, and Emotional Problems: Health of Our Nation's Children, United States, 1988*. Hyattsville, MD: National Center for Health Statistics, 1990, p. 9.

27 Steven Pinker, *How the Mind Works*. New York: W. W. Norton, 2009, p. 434.

Notes to pp. 127–135

28 Martin Daly and Margo Wilson, 'The 'Cinderella effect' is no fairy tale', *Trends in Cognitive Sciences* 9 (2005): 507–8.

29 Quoted in Diane Jeske and Richard Fumerton, eds, *Readings in Political Philosophy: Theory and Applications.* Peterborough, Ont.: Broadview Press, 2011, p. 649.

30 *The Hostel for Homeless Young Mums*, episode 1, BBC3, 7 June 2019.

31 Barbara A. Crow, *Radical Feminism: A Documentary Reader.* New York: New York University Press, 2000, p. 76.

32 Amy Westervelt, 26 May 2018, https://www.theguardian.com/commentisfree/2018/may/26/is-motherhood-the-unfinished-work-of-feminism.

33 https://slate.com/human-interest/2013/06/female-academics-pay-a-heavy-baby-penalty.html.

34 *As You Like It*, Act II, scene VII.

35 https://www.thepublicdiscourse.com/2011/03/2638/.

36 Eli J. Finkel, *The All-or-Nothing Marriage: How the Best Marriages Work.* New York: Dutton, 2017.

37 Erika Bachiochi, *The Rights of Women: Reclaiming a Lost Vision.* Notre Dame, IN: University of Notre Dame Press, 2021, p. 16.

38 D. R. White, L. Betzig, M. B. Mulder et al., 'Rethinking polygyny: co-wives, codes, and cultural systems' (and comments and reply), *Current Anthropology* 29 (1988): 529–72; www.jstor.org/stable/2743506.

39 Henrich, Joseph, Robert Boyd and Peter J Richerson. 'The puzzle of monogamous marriage.' *Philosophical Transactions of the Royal Society B: Biological Sciences* 367, no. 1589 (2012): 657–69.

Notes to pp. 137–144

40 Lee Gettler, Thomas McDade, Alan Feranil and Christopher Kuzawa, 'Longitudinal evidence that fatherhood decreases testosterone in human males', *Proceedings of the National Academy of Sciences of the United States of America* 108 (2011): 16194–9.

Conclusion: Listen to Your Mother

1 See https://defaultfriend.substack.com/p/72-the-coming -wave-of-sex-negativity/comments.
2 https://www.tiktok.com/@vyvansemommy/video/ 7005669146797100294.

ACKNOWLEDGEMENTS

I owe enormous thanks to my agent, Matthew Hamilton, and my editor, George Owers, without whom the original edition of this book would never have been written. I am also indebted to the many people who read and commented on various proposals and drafts of the original book: Julie Bindel, Diana Fleischman, David Goodhart, Camille Guillot, Jessica Masterson, Dina McMillan, Nina Power, Katharina Rietzler, Rajiv Shah, Kathleen Stock and Randy Thornhill. I owe particular thanks to the brilliant Mary Harrington, who provided constant support and ideas, and to my other feminist friends: Alex Kaschuta, Katherine Dee, Helen Roy and Mason Hartman. I am eternally grateful to Fiona MacKenzie, my friend and colleague, who founded *We Can't Consent To This*. And I owe thanks also to Eve and Max for sticking by me, despite my terrible opinions – I really do appreciate it.

Acknowledgements

I depend, as ever, on the love and companionship of my husband and family, including my beloved son, who was born during the writing of the original book, and my most faithful reader, my mum, who has read every word I've ever published.